Religious Minority Students in Higher Education

The most recent addition to the *Key Issues on Diverse College Students* series bridges theory to practice in order to help student affairs and higher education professionals understand the needs and experiences of religious minorities on college campuses. *Religious Minority Students in Higher Education* explores existing literature and research on religious minorities on American college campuses, discusses the challenges and needs of religious minorities on campus, and provides best practices and recommendations. Providing a foundational, nuanced approach to religious minorities in the American college context, this important resource will help educators at colleges and universities promote religious pluralism and tolerance to support student learning outcomes and campus inclusion among students of diverse religious backgrounds.

Yoruba T. Mutakabbir is Assistant Professor of Higher Education at Texas Southern University, USA.

Tariqah A. Nuriddin is Assistant Professor of Sociology at Howard University, USA.

KEY ISSUES ON DIVERSE COLLEGE STUDENTS

Series Editors: Marybeth Gasman and Nelson Bowman III

Asian American Students in Higher Education
Samuel D. Museus

Black Men in Higher Education: A Guide to Ensuring Student Success
J. Luke Wood and Robert T. Palmer

Student Veterans and Service Members in Higher Education
Jan Arminio, Tomoko Kudo Grabosky, and Josh Lang

Religious Minority Students in Higher Education
Yoruba T. Mutakabbir and Tariqah A. Nuriddin

Religious Minority Students in Higher Education

Yoruba T. Mutakabbir
Tariqah A. Nuriddin

Routledge
Taylor & Francis Group

NEW YORK AND LONDON

First published 2016
by Routledge
711 Third Avenue, New York, NY 10017

and by Routledge
2 Park Square, Milton Park, Abingdon, Oxon, OX14 4RN

Routledge is an imprint of the Taylor & Francis Group, an informa business

© 2016 Taylor & Francis

The right of Yoruba T. Mutakabbir and Tariqah A. Nuriddin to be identified as authors of this work has been asserted by them in accordance with sections 77 and 78 of the Copyright, Designs and Patents Act 1988.

Library of Congress Cataloging in Publication Data
A catalog record for this book has been requested

ISBN: 978-1-138-82083-8 (hbk)
ISBN: 978-1-138-82084-5 (pbk)
ISBN: 978-1-315-74365-3 (ebk)

Typeset in Sabon and Bell Gothic
by Wearset Ltd, Boldon, Tyne and Wear

Printed and bound in the United States of America by
Edwards Brothers Malloy on sustainably sourced paper

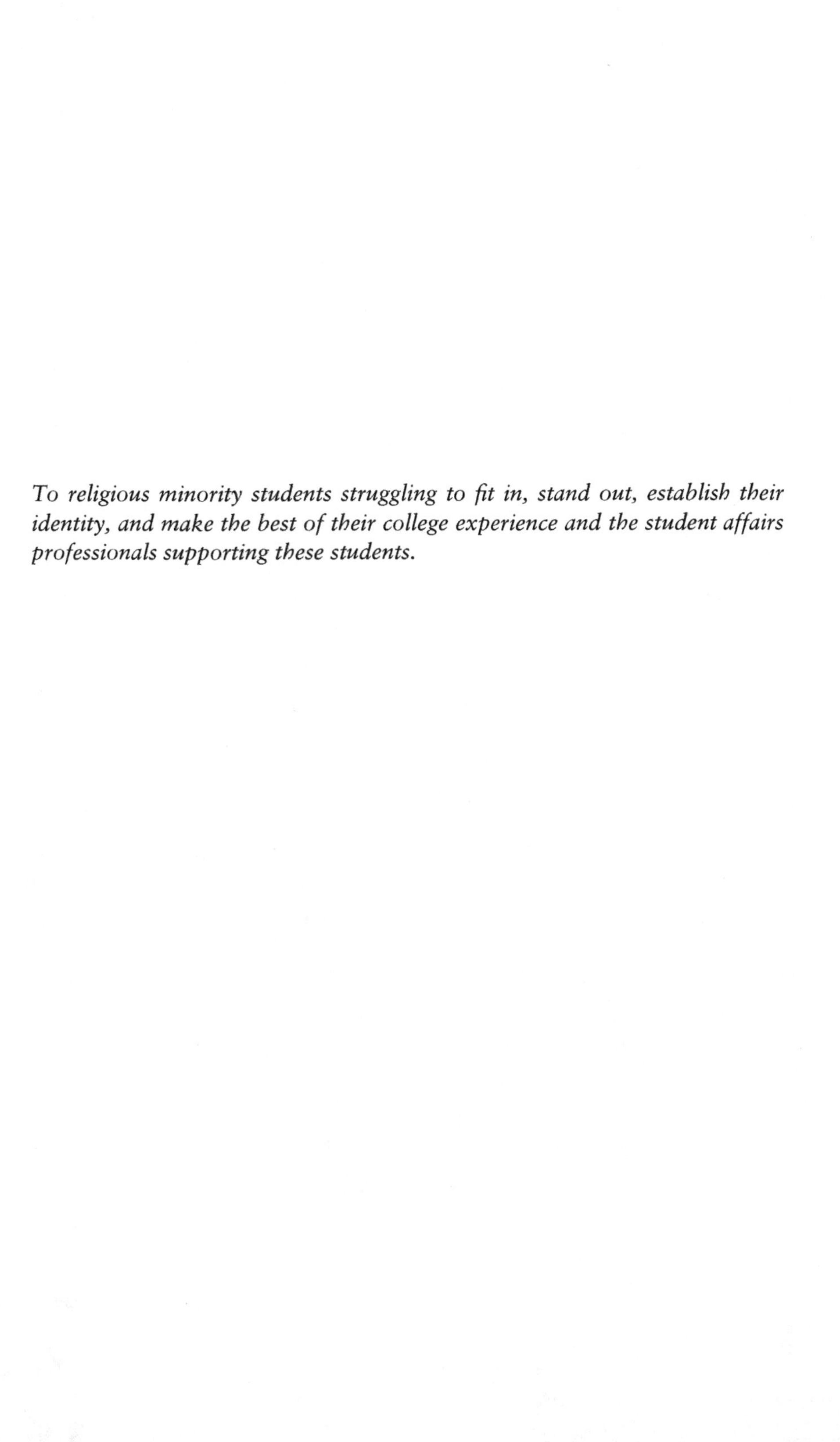

To religious minority students struggling to fit in, stand out, establish their identity, and make the best of their college experience and the student affairs professionals supporting these students.

Contents

Figures

Tables

Series Editors' Introduction

We are excited about the inclusion of Yoruba T. Mutakabbir and Tariqah A. Nuriddin's book *Religious Minority Students in Higher Education* in our Key Issues on Diverse College Students series with Routledge Press.

Although diversity is discussed at length in higher education literature, religion is often left out of these discussions because people are sometimes uncomfortable talking about religion, it is not always seen as a form of student diversity, and it is under studied by scholars of higher education in general.

Mutakabbir and Nuriddin's book is particularly interesting because they lived through the experience of being religious minorities in college. They know firsthand the discrimination that students can feel when they don't conform to religious norms in belief, dress, diet, or custom. This personal knowledge, along with a deep understanding of the research, has produced a book that is both scholarly in its approach and practical in nature.

Student affairs practitioners as well as academics will gain immensely from reading it, as the recommendations are timely, sensitive, and doable. Mutakabbir and Nuriddin not only provide guidance on assessing campus religious climates, but they also offer strategies for meeting the diverse and sometimes delicate needs of religious minorities.

Perhaps the most profound aspect of the book is that Mutakabbir and Nuriddin make a plea to college and university administration to embrace religious pluralism in the same ways that they have worked to embrace racial and ethnic pluralism.

We hope you will learn a great deal from *Religious Minority Students in Higher Education*. We certainly did.

Marybeth Gasman and Nelson Bowman III
Series Editors

Preface

This book was inspired by our personal experiences as religious minority (Muslim) college students. Although we had a satisfying college experience at the Historically Black College (HBCU) we attended, our undergraduate institution left much to be desired in terms of religious inclusion. We dealt with issues such as mandatory chapel attendance during freshman orientation, religiously biased dress code regulations, and the unavailability of food service during Ramadan. Working on this project carries special meaning for us since we have experienced what it is like to feel less than included on a college campus due to our religion.

Religious Minority Students in Higher Education addresses the challenges of religious minority students on college campuses. We define and discuss who is a religious minority and how that definition may vary from campus to campus. Extant research on religious minority college students, though minimal, is discussed as well. Student affairs personnel and administrators are the primary audience for this book. For student affairs professionals who are struggling with understanding the various religions, spiritual beliefs, and worldviews, this text can serve as a guide for accommodating students of such backgrounds. In order to serve students, student affairs personnel must first know students. Understanding students' religious, spiritual background or worldview is an integral part of knowing them. However, faculty, students, and anyone interested in religious diversity and/or college student experiences may find this book interesting. Strategies for meeting the needs of religious minority students, assessing campus religious climate, and implementing religion into diversity strategic plans are also reviewed in this text.

This book is comprised of six chapters. The opening chapter provides an overview of religious minority college students. We define who is a religious minority in an American context and frame religious pluralism in the context of college student affairs. The second chapter consists of a review of the literature on religious minority college students. In Chapter 3, we discuss methods for campus climate assessment, such as surveys and focus groups. Classroom contexts are the focus of Chapter 4. Even though student affairs deals with student experiences outside of the classroom, the classroom can play an integral role in validating religious minorities. In Chapter 5, we discuss campus accommodation and address what religious minorities need to comfortably practice their faith on campus. Specifically discussed are the availability of interfaith prayer/meditation rooms, kosher, halal, and/or vegetarian dietary offerings, headgear regulations, and chaplain service. The concluding chapter provides student affairs practitioners and administrators with recommendations for practice. Suggestions for future research and the intersection of race and religion are also discussed. Specifically, suggestions for facilitating difficult discussions on religious diversity and a list of professional competencies needed to address religious diversity are shared in this chapter.

Diversity is a prolific buzz word within higher education. However, the word *diversity* primarily conjures up dialogue on race, gender, or LGBTQ issues. We hope this book will encourage the addition of religion to the discourse on diversity in higher education. Despite the differences between racial issues and religious issues, colleges should promote religious pluralism and tolerance with the same effort and resources as multiculturalism and racial diversity.

Acknowledgments

Yoruba: I would like to thank my parents, Tamir and Teresa Mutakabbir, for providing me with a spiritual foundation and their support. I am also thankful for the support of other family, friends, and colleagues.

Tariqah: First and foremost, I would like to thank the Creator for blessing me with such a rich and full life. There have been numerous twists and turns along the way, but I suppose this has served to fortify my character and conviction. Next, I would like to thank my parents, Jalal and Habibah, for pouring their love and kindness into my being. I also would like to thank my loving husband, Muhammad, daughter Sarah Safia, loving siblings and family members, supportive friends, phenomenal past teachers/professors, and students (both current and former) for all of their support over the years. A very special recognition of gratitude goes to the staff at the Louis Stokes Health Sciences Library, my research study group partners, Yolonda and Brandon, and my former student Angelo Pereira for his pedagogical contributions to the book. I would also like to thank the four Muslim male students who supplied us with interviews for our research project. I also would like to expressly thank my co-author, Dr. Yoruba Mutakabbir for her friendship, dedication, and hard work toward this entire book project. Last, but certainly not least, I would like to thank the Routledge production team for their patience and ability to see the value in our vision.

Chapter 1

Introduction

A personal story largely illustrates what powerful forces education and religion are. My mother-in-law is a 70-year-old African-American Muslim convert. She was born in 1945, raised as a Christian and part of the famous baby boom generation. During one of our many conversations, she mentioned to me what it was like growing up in New Jersey as a kid. One thing that struck me was when she told me that all she knew was Christianity. She had never even heard of Islam or Muslims until the 1960s. It was almost as if the religion of Islam did not exist. In her world, it surely was not present. She completed school but never had heard of the religion of Islam. It may be hard to believe this story in the world we live in now, but it is true. We all know that there are places in America where no one has ever even met a Buddhist, Hindu, Sikh or Muslim and where people have no clear conception of these religions except what they may or may not see in the media. Education must be transformative not stifling. As a nation settled by immigrants and built by slave labor, America still lives in her past but must move forward in order to survive.

EDUCATION AND RELIGION AS SOCIAL INSTITUTIONS

As the opening caveat suggests, colleges and universities are first and foremost institutions. Yet, so is religion. Both do not exist in a vacuum but rather fundamentally shape almost every aspect of our social lives. Education and religion may influence our values, beliefs, inter and intrapersonal relationships, dietary rules, social cohesion, and marital preferences. From a sociological perspective, it is our institutions which socialize individuals from birth until death and have enormous generational effects given their stature in our society and the subsequent power they are able to wield on both individuals and groups. Power is the ability to get someone to do something you want them to do, either willingly or unwillingly. The institutions of education and religion are powerful forces in American society. Most Americans are connected to one or both of these institutions for a large part, if not all, of their lives.

SOCIAL FUNCTIONS OF EDUCATION AND RELIGION

As mentioned above, both education and religion have the primary function of the socialization of individuals to their social environments. The second function of education is to produce individuals with socially desirable traits in order that they become productive members of society. Lastly, the third function of education is to groom students for their adult roles (Eitzen & Zinn, 1997). Education has many distinct characteristics in the United States. Among them are the following: 1) Conservatism; 2) Mass education; 3) Local control; 4) Competition; 5) The sifting and sorting function of schools; and 6) The preoccupation with order and control (Eitzen & Zinn, 1997).

The problem with the social functions and features of education is that students are often perceived to be innocent bystanders to the educational onslaught and are encouraged to always follow the rules and procedures for maximum benefit. In this sense, institutional education often breeds uniformity but not necessarily innovation. Just like religious deviants, educational deviants may be put in detention, suspended, or even expelled for going against the grain. Thus, as institutions, both education and religion may be reluctant to change, but without change, the likelihood of growth diminishes significantly.

Religion can be defined as a set of core beliefs about the nature of the sacred or supernatural, which may be combined with symbols and rituals which tie people together as a collective group (Kendall, 2000). Social functions of religion include: 1) The provision of meaning and purpose; 2) Social cohesion and a sense of belonging (McGuire, 1997); and 3) Social control and support for the government (Geertz, 1966). These functions should not be underestimated and are very important for many persons to feel that they are a part of something bigger or larger than themselves. Just as sports fans may feel a deep connection with other fans who are strangers across the United States, or the world for that matter, persons who are members of religious "teams" may feel a sense of comradery and belonging that may be difficult to explain.

When it comes to our colleges and universities in America, many factors may be shaped by religious preferences and culture. Colleges and universities serve the important social function of training young adults to have the skills and expertise to enter the workforce, among other important skills. Despite the enormous task of the education of young adults, colleges and universities may also provide meal plans, dormitory accommodation, courses, facilities, student groups, and campus ministries, which also may serve to promote or hinder campus spiritual life. The question may be asked if colleges and universities across America are equipped to handle the responsibility of not only education but social cohesion, safety, pluralism, academic freedom and, most importantly, a critical ideological and ethical dialogue of inclusion over exclusion. The answer is that our institutions have a long way to go; however, the stakes are too high and education cannot afford to be non-innovative, non-inclusive, and irrelevant (Woolbright, 1989).

Besides the formal education of students, colleges and universities across America have their own unique cultures and campus atmospheres associated with them. From conservative to liberal campuses and everything in between, there is a veritable cornucopia of options for the would-be college student to select from. Besides finding a university that is affordable and has a strong academic program in their field of study, students may also be interested in how they will fit into the social fabrics of their respective universities and geographical locations they will be residing in for the next four to five years of their lives. For an individual who occupies the status of religious minority, the choice of college selection may prove to be even greater. College selection is indeed one of the most important and far-reaching life decisions a student may make (Hossler, Schmit, & Vesper, 1999). Of the many factors that may lead to college selection, the fit of the school, comfort, and level of acceptance have been shown to play a pivotal role for both minority and non-minority students (Nora, 2004).

Harvard University is among one of the oldest universities in the United States and has been around since 1636; initially as Harvard College (Harvard University, 2015; Waggoner, 2011). Interestingly enough, it was initially founded as a school to train and educate clergy members and later changed from this approach as time passed and in order to accommodate the shifts in the colonial mindset. In contrast, in the case of many newer public colleges and universities, religion was not the focus but rather other seemingly more important areas, such as philosophy and science.

It should be noted that many of the premier educational institutions in America were created out of a premise of exclusion since formal schooling was not free and public education did not exist until much later. Thus, for well over two centuries, education in America was primarily for the elite, not the masses. The non-wealthy, females, and persons of color were largely excluded and ignored from the foundations of education. In the 2013 book *Ebony and Ivy*, author Craig Steven Wilder discusses how enslaved Africans were sent with their masters or the children of their masters to serve them while at school at prominent universities across the country, such as Harvard, Yale, and the like. These very same institutions of higher education used slave labor to build the facilities and service the universities' patrons. Conversion of Native Americans to Christianity was also seen as carrying out the purpose of education. Here we see the early historical inextricable link between religion and education, although it did not start out on good terms.

Thus, from its earliest onset, American higher education was not necessarily intended or built for everyone and those that had the resources and wherewithal to be educated formed members of an already elite and privileged few. Neil Postman reiterated this point in his book *The End of Education: Redefining the Value of School* by the following excerpt:

> America has always been a nation of nations, our schools always multicultural. But educators have not always been concerned to emphasize this fact, in part because of the belief that through schooling a common culture could be created; in part because immigrant cultures were thought to be inferior to Anglo-Saxon cultures.
>
> (Postman, 1996, p. 74)

As time passed and American culture changed from being more exclusionary to more embracing, the institutions of higher education have had to confront the enormous issue of diversity and inclusion in contrast to homogeneity and exclusion. In a 1922 article entitled "Harvard Student Opinion on the Jewish Question," Harvard students shared their concerns regarding the perceived influx of Jewish students into the university and the perceived negative impact this had on the future of the institution (Ham, 1922). This was most likely the rule not the exception at the time.

Michael Waggoner, in his book entitled *Sacred and Secular Tensions in Higher Education*, suggests that, if we fast forward to the modern day, there is more of a balkanization of religion on campus. This balkanization refers to the following result on many campuses: "a collection of interested parties with limited reach and effectiveness." Waggoner argues that the sacred and the secular should have a place at the academic dinner table through competition as to whom has the most viable ideas rather than by default. Although institutions of higher education have largely secular leanings, this does not mean that the sacred has no place.

Notions of how to intermingle the sacred with the secular are part of the long history of America and discussions will continue to evolve and grow as the American population continues to diversify. One thing is clear: in order to move forward, more conversations need to be made with the common goal of mutual understanding.

RELIGIOUS DIVERSITY IN HIGHER EDUCATION

It should be noted that the topic of religious diversity at institutions of higher education may be seemingly innocuous but it is both highly controversial and political. Under the section on Integrative Diverse Populations, sociologist Joan Ferrante suggests that

> Schools function to integrate (for example, to Americanize or Europeanize) people of different, ethnic, racial, religious, and family backgrounds. In the United States, schools play a significant role in what is known as the melting-pot process. Recall that the "peopling of America is one of the greatest dramas in all of human history" (Sowell, 1981, p. 3). It involved the conquest of the native peoples, the annexation of Mexican territory along with many of its inhabitants (who lived in what is now New Mexico, Utah, Nevada, Arizona, California, and parts of Colorado and Texas), and an influx of millions of people from practically every country in the world. Early American school reformers – primarily those of Protestant and British backgrounds – saw public education as the vehicle for Americanizing a culturally and linguistically diverse population, instilling a sense of national unity and purpose, and training a competent workforce.
>
> (Ferrante, 2008, p. 369)

YES, WE CAN?

Affirmative action policies which came out of the civil rights movement in essence forced universities to diversify their student populations despite their hesitance. The demise of legal segregation in the United States has had a tremendous impact on public education in this country. It has not only increased the racial and ethnic composition of students at public institutions, but fundamentally changed the culture in America through less stringent immigration policies which allowed for racial and ethnic minorities from other countries to study in the United States. Today, opponents of affirmative action policies might say that they give unfair or undue preference to minority students over seemingly qualified White student applicants. This viewpoint is problematic in that it attempts to ignore the social and cultural conditions which have led to the increasingly vast educational gap between White, Black, and Native American students. A gap that is not closing but perhaps even widening as we speak. There is an elephant in the room and it is massive in scope and scale, but for some reason, we choose to ignore it. America is caught in a schism between those who identify with the old way of doing things as opposed to those who envision a new America. Ultimately, America still has one foot in the past and one foot in the present, which may have deleterious effects on the discipline of education in this country if this thinking is not adjusted.

Table 1.1 represents just how far America has come in the past century. The America of old (left column) was much more exclusionary and resistant to change. However, there were some good traits, such as infrastructure investment and a largely indigenous workforce. The America of today (right column) has had significant gains in racial and economic equality. However, due to the century's long foothold of old America, many things have sadly stayed very much the same or close to it. The political, economic, and global power structure is still a virtually all White male dominated enterprise. Although there have been some improvements, the spheres of work are still highly gendered, not just in terms of profession (i.e., nursing, teaching,

Table 1.1 Old America Characteristics vs. New America Characteristics

Old America Characteristics	New America Characteristics
Racial and ethnic segregation	Racial and ethnic integration
Homogeneity preferred	Heterogeneity preferred
Rampant racism, sexism, and misogyny	Non-discriminatory policy against gender, age, racial, ethnic, and religious minorities, persons with disabilities, and sexual orientation
Miscegenation outlawed	Miscegenation tolerated
Trade and vocation focused	Technology and service oriented
De jure segregation	De facto segregation
Virtually all White male power structure	Virtually all White male power structure with limited inclusion of women and persons of color
Clear delineation between men's work and women's work	Lines between men and women's work are more obscure
Limited global political engagement and diplomatic relationships	High global political engagement and diplomatic relationships
Economic investment in social welfare and infrastructure, such as highways, dams, bridges, etc.	Economic investment in military expenditures
Indigenous workforce	Outsourced workforce
Low-level access to basic public education which teaches basic skills	High access to higher education which teaches advanced and specialized skills
Basic curriculum with limited course offerings	Advanced curriculum with many course offerings

Note: Some characteristics from the list were based on Thomas McBride's (2011) book entitled *The Mindset Lists of American History: From Typewriters to Text Messages, What Ten Generations of Americans Think Is Normal.*

construction), but also in terms of administrative positions. In the field of higher education, it is well documented that females tend to occupy the status of non-tenure track jobs or Assistant Professorships to a greater degree than their male counterparts (Ginther & Hayes, 2003). Unfortunately, the student loan debt burden for students is over one trillion dollars, with many students insecure about whether they will even receive a job following graduation (Denhart, 2013).

In terms of the good news, races and ethnicities are more integrated now than ever before in this country as a result of the Civil Rights Act of 1964. Although the practice of discrimination is outlawed, this does not mean that it does not take place. We need only look at the cultural events of the past few years where countless unarmed Black teens/adults were killed by largely White male police officers.

Yet there are still many steeped in the traditions of old America. Alas, they are a dying breed. What will the future of education hold for minorities and religious minorities in particular? Only time will tell.

DIVERSITY

Initially, the topic of diversity started out with a discussion of race since American colleges and universities were segregated primarily based on this social construct. The applications of old requested students to send pictures so their skin color and phenotype could be used to determine if they were the "right fit" for the college or university in question.

Diversity is a buzz word in a modern-day sense with many progressive institutions suggesting that they have a diverse student body. But what does diversity really mean? Are institutions of higher learning as diverse as they proclaim they are? Perhaps a working definition of diversity should be explained to get us started. The University of Oregon's Office of Diversity Initiatives states the following for its definition of diversity:

> The concept of diversity encompasses acceptance and respect. It means understanding that each individual is unique, and recognizing our individual differences. These can be along the dimensions of race, ethnicity, gender, sexual orientation, socio-economic status, age, physical disabilities, religious beliefs, political beliefs, or other ideologies. It is the exploration of these differences in a safe, positive, and nurturing environment. It is about understanding each other and moving beyond simple tolerance to embracing and celebrating the rich dimensions of diversity contained within each individual.
>
> (The University of Oregon, 2015)

Although this definition may sound a bit idealistic, its merit is one rooted in respect and inclusion. Far too often, diversity is assumed if there is variation of race, religion, and socio-economic status. However, to truly achieve diversity, voices should not only be tolerated but given a say in the decision-making process. Colleges and universities in the United States have the ability and are uniquely positioned to really move toward the creation of campus climates that truly embody diversity without paying just mere lip service to the idea. However, since our educational institutions are microcosms of larger society, we still find quite a bit of separation in our institutions of higher education.

As America diversifies, universities now more than ever are moving toward the diversification of their student body. What is often unclear is the viability of the method that will be used to accomplish such a task. In a landmark Supreme Court decision in 2003, it was ruled that the University of Michigan could not allot points to undergraduate applicants based on race (Rhone, 2006). Many schools were left befuddled in terms of how to increase their numbers and racial and gender minority students in terms of undergraduate admission. In 2006, Harvard came up with a plan to divvy out scholarships with the announcement that students whose families had incomes of $60,000 or less would be given free tuition. Other strategies include using a combination of factors, such as financial considerations, life circumstances, and first-generation college student status (Rhone, 2006). Just as colleges and universities seek to diversify by race, gender, and income; should colleges also seek to diversify by religion? If so, in which ways could a potential student's religious perspective serve to add to a particular program or major? Likewise, what are the consequences of not diversifying by religion in terms of a rigorous education which challenges students to confront perspectives they may or may not be exposed to?

Munce (2005) argues that colleges and universities are not doing enough to diversify their student body. Despite the *Grutter* v. *Bollinger* Supreme Court decision, which allowed for universities to expand admissions opportunities to students of various racial backgrounds, not all universities have taken advantage. Munce suggests that many universities are not truly serious about diversity. As such, students that are already represented on campus tend to be overrepresented in college admissions decisions. More specifically, males, students from socio-economically disadvantaged backgrounds, African-Americans, and Native Americans continue to be underrepresented.

Slight changes to admissions criteria may significantly improve and diversify the selection pool of applicants. Strategies such as slightly lowering the grade point average requirement by one letter grade (e.g., A– to a B+) and greater solicitation of college materials to racial minority households may serve as a step in the right direction (Munce, 2005). Likewise, universities which are serious about diversity are even utilizing the new equity scorecard created by the Center for Urban Education to assess levels of racial equity on campus. This scorecard allows for not only the identification but potential eradication of racial disparities in educational outcomes on college campuses (Harris III & Bensimon, 2007; Bensimon & Malcolm, 2012).

RELIGIOUS DIVERSITY

When it comes to the topic of religious diversity, the United States is usually considered a religiously diverse country since there are millions of persons across the religious spectrum. However, according to data from the Pew Research Center, the United States is not as religiously diverse as it may appear. In comparison to other industrialized countries such as Singapore and France, the United States ranked only moderately based on the religious diversity index, which ranges from very high to low. According to the Pew study, 78% of Americans fall under the umbrella of Christianity, 16% remain unaffiliated, and the remaining 6% fall under the remaining religious categories (Islam, Hinduism, Buddhism, Folk Religions, Other Religions, and Jews) (Table 1.2). The Pew Study results are consistent with the work of Smith (2002), who found that, although the numbers of religious minorities in this country are steadily increasing, the sheer proportions and expansion of primarily Buddhist, Hindu and Muslim religious minorities are sometimes overstated. According to Francis Fukuyama (1994), the idea that there is some sort of menacing immigrant invasion from other cultures that is set to replace America's Christian European roots is false. In fact, Fukuyama argues that the national identity of America has never been linked to just one singular ethnicity or particular religion, which distinguishes America from many of its counterparts.

Table 1.2 Four Levels of Religious Diversity (%)

	Singapore	France	United States	Iran
Christians	18	63	78	<1
Muslims	14	8	<1	99
Unaffiliated	16	28	16	<1
Hindus	5	<1	<1	<1
Buddhists	34	<1	1	<1
Folk Religions	2	<1	<1	<1
Other Religions	10	<1	<1	<1
Jews	<1	<1	2	<1

For the purposes of our discussion, religious minorities are defined as those groups who have traditionally experienced some level of economic, social, and political subjugation as a result of their religion and other presumed attributes.

RELIGIOUS MINORITY

When we use the term religious minority we do not necessarily mean in numerical terms. Based on the discussion of Taylor (2002), a minority constitutes a "status designation" which corresponds to unequal access to economic, political, and social resources and opportunities within a given society. In contrast, a majority group refers to a group who has economic, social, and political resources at their disposal and has attained both power and prestige as a result of these privileges. For example, a Catholic student at a Catholic University would constitute a religious majority even if Catholic students were fewer in number than other religious groups on campus. As a Catholic University, the university is catered toward such students, which creates a built-in privilege. In contrast, aside from Zaytuna College in California, most Muslim college students would be religious minorities at their respective universities.

CHRISTIAN PRIVILEGE

The spiritual enhancement of all faith groups on college campuses should be pursued by administration as a must. One of the potential barriers to the spiritual growth of students of all faith backgrounds is Christian privilege (Seifert, 2007). Christian privilege can be defined as "the conscious and subconscious advantages often afforded to the Christian faith in America's colleges and universities" (Seifert, 2007, p. 11). The failure to acknowledge dominant religious privilege on campus may lead to the inadvertent subjugation of minority religious groups. Despite the relaxed religious atmosphere on college campuses for the past century, Christianity is not only dominant but pervasive. Christian privilege can take the form of Christmas holiday breaks, a central chapel location on campus, biased institutional calendars, dining menu selections, Monday through Friday work week, holiday parties, no physical space on campus to practice one's religion, Christian-based commencement prayers, and discrimination due to wearing religious attire (e.g., hijab, turban). The steps to remedy Christian privilege are to: 1) accept that it exists; 2) address it; 3) advocate a culture of mutual respect for all faith groups; and 4) create groups where students can openly dialogue and learn from each other.

Countries with high levels of religious diversity are pushed to tackle issues of assimilation head on. For example, France has a high religious diversity index and a sizeable immigrant population, who are considered by many to be marginalized in French ghettoes. In the past few years in France, there has been a push toward the assimilation of religious minorities as reflected by the law. In 2004, French citizens who attend public schools were banned from wearing any religious symbols or paraphernalia. This included crosses (Christian), yarmulkes (Jewish male head covering), kufis (Muslim male head covering), hijabs (Muslim female head covering), turbans (Sikh male head covering), and so forth (Scott, 2007).

While some may have praised the move by France to take a firm position, taking the sacred out of public schools, others saw it as an attack on the religious freedoms of students. Especially that of Muslim female students who are required to cover their hair and dress modestly. Due to France's sizeable Muslim population (e.g., Algerians, etc.), such a move could lead to further feelings of isolation on the part of French Muslim immigrants. With the recent Charlie Hebdo massacre, it appears that extreme elements of the French Muslim population may feel as if they are overly marginalized based on their religion.

However, France is not alone in terms of the hijab ban. Other countries in Europe have also instituted some type of restriction on hijab, such as Italy, Turkey, Belgium, Amsterdam, Germany, and Canada, but none are as extreme as the French ban. Predominantly Muslim countries such as Turkey also adopted the hijab ban in public spaces (such as schools and civil service occupations), but this has now been lifted. We are likely not to see the end of such practices as Europe also continues to diversify (Smith, 2013).

Such occurrences are a sad but true reality that there is an ever-growing anti-immigrant rhetoric that pervades social and political circles. One need only look at the largely negative rhetoric directed toward Mexicans and Central Americans in search of better opportunities and the corresponding Arizona laws which follow suit. According to Cornel West:

> Our history shows that stirring the deep commitment to democratic values and mandates does make a difference. But we must not confuse this democratic commitment with flag-waving patriotism. The former is guided by common virtues forged by ordinary citizens, the latter by martial ideals promoted by powerful elites. Democratic commitment confronts American hypocrisy and mendacity in the name of public interest; flag-waving patriotism promotes American innocence and purity in the name of national glory.
>
> (West, 2005, p. 103)

Despite the separation of church and state in the United States, religion tremendously shapes the public and private lives of the American public. America is undergoing important demographic shifts that will fundamentally shape the course of its history. Just like when we embraced the concept of mass public education in the past, America is uniquely positioned to be at the forefront of innovative pedagogical changes in this country. In order to accomplish this task, textbooks must be revisited; public education curriculums must reflect the growing diversity of the American public. We can no longer afford to stay isolated and ignorant of other cultures and global affairs.

HIGHER EDUCATION AND CURRICULUM ADJUSTMENTS

Universities are realizing that, in order to become global, top-ranking schools, they must have diverse course offerings. In order to offer an array of different courses, universities must also be willing and able to attract faculty members who are equipped to teach such classes. Institutions, colleges, and universities may be resistant to change, but if the large majority of one's students are from a particular racial/ethnic or religious background, they may need to rethink the sanctity of their curriculum. New York University, for instance, has satellite campuses in Abu Dhabi and Beijing. NYU prides itself on creating a new world-class education. In order to accomplish such a tremendous endeavor, diversity and student engagement seems to be at the forefront. This new model for campus life and curriculum may include a plethora of various campus activities, events, and courses which speak to diversity and pluralism on campus.

IMPORTANCE OF RELIGIOUS DIVERSITY IN HIGHER EDUCATION

There are several reasons why it is important to understand religious minorities and religious diversity in higher education.

1. *Social fabric.* Religious minorities make up the fabric of America and are important to the American educational and cultural landscape. In order for American institutions of higher education to truly advance, they must embrace religious diversity. During his political campaign, President Obama was accused of being a closet Muslim and un-American. In response, former secretary of state Colin Powell stated:

   > Well, the correct answer is, he is not a Muslim, he's a Christian. He's always been a Christian. But the really right answer is, what if he is? Is there something wrong with being a Muslim in this country? The

> answer's no, that's not America. Is there something wrong with some seven-year-old Muslim-American kid believing that he or she could be president? Yet, I have heard senior members of my own party drop the suggestion, "He's a Muslim and he might be associated with terrorists." This is not the way we should be doing it in America.
>
> (Johnson, 2012)

On a related note, Congressman Keith Ellison swore his oath of office on Thomas Jefferson's copy of the Qur'an. Upon hearing the news, many Americans were flabbergasted that Thomas Jefferson knew anything about Islam, let alone owned a personal copy of the Qur'an. The point is that an authentic American should not be viewed as a particular race or religion. The original indigenous persons of this country (Native Americans) only currently represent about 1% of the ethnic make-up of America (Schaefer, 2011). Everyone else came by force or by choice over several generations or just recently due to shifts in U.S. immigration policy. The home we call America is moving toward further diversity, not less. The sooner we come to terms with this, the better.

2. *Religious intolerance.* Many hate crimes in America are not only directed toward racial minorities by religious minorities as well. Ignorance of and cultural separation from other religious groups may lead to prejudiced attitudes or discrimination directed toward religious minorities. For example, after September 11, 2011, there was a spike in arrests and hate crimes directed toward visible racial and religious minorities, such as Muslims and Hindus (Nguyen, 2005; Donahue, 2002). Unfortunately, even our nation's institutions of higher learning were not immune from such acts. If acts of hatred due to religious intolerance persist in our highly educated environments, what of those environments that are highly racially and ethnically segregated and perhaps less open to discussions of diversity?

3. *Religious pluralism.* America has the unique opportunity to move toward pluralism in the next few decades. If we examine the global religious landscape, we find that Islam, Hinduism, Buddhism, Sikhism, and Judaism have several billion followers. Thus, even though Christianity is the world's largest religion, the majority of the world is non-Christian. Yet, how much does the average American know about global faiths other than Christianity, other than what they are taught in schools (if any) or via the media? If our institutions of higher education do not get it right, American college students will miss out on an important opportunity to become intellectually and politically savvy individuals who live in a complex global world. American culture is not monolithic and neither is the globe.

Few studies exist which attempt to understand the plight of religious minorities on campus. The current book represents a modest attempt to explore this topic in further detail and provide suggestions for moving forward. Without a clear understanding of the nature of the problem, viable solutions will not be made.

The next chapter will discuss existing literature on religious minorities enrolled in college. Also discussed in this chapter will be literature on campus multifaith/interfaith initiatives, specifically, literature on Jewish, Muslim, Animist and other religious minorities. Gaps in the literature will be highlighted and suggestions are offered for future research.

DISCUSSION QUESTIONS

1. How do education and religion represent powerful social institutions? How have these institutions been powerful in your own life?
2. What are the social functions of education and religion? Are there any other functions of education that you would want to add to the list?
3. Should colleges and universities have non-educational related responsibilities? If so, how can they make it easier and more educationally relevant for their students?
4. What are the factors that lead students to select a college or university to attend?
5. What is the historical link between education and religion in America? Who was education intended for? Which groups were initially excluded from education?
6. Should religious studies courses be included in the curriculum of both public and private universities? If so, what types of courses should be included in the curriculum?
7. Why would early schools attempt to "Americanize" persons of different racial and ethnic backgrounds? Are remnants of this culture prevalent in the schools of today?
8. Based on the characteristics of old America versus new America, what do you think education was like for different racial, ethnic, and gender groups under each system?
9. Why does the concept of diversity need to expand beyond having a few more people of color in the room?
10. Argue the pros and cons of America becoming a more religiously diverse country.
11. Why is it important to have religious diversity in higher education?
12. In what ways might the social status you occupy (i.e., gender, race, ethnicity, socio-economic status) make you more or less privileged in the classroom setting?

13. Informally interview a member of a religious minority group. Ask the student the following three questions: "How do you think being a student at this school has impacted your religious faith and practice?", "What obstacles have you encountered in the practice of your faith while at school?", and "How did you overcome those obstacles (if at all)?" In order to push yourself even further, you may want to interview persons of different faith backgrounds and compare your results.

REFERENCES

Bensimon, E.M., & Malcolm, L. (2012). *Confronting Equity Issues on Campus: Implementing the Equity Scorecard in Theory and Practice*. Sterling, VA: Stylus Pub.

Denhart, C. (2013, August 7). How the $1.2 trillion college debt crisis is crippling students, parents and the economy. *Forbes*. Retrieved from: www.forbes.com/sites/specialfeatures/2013/08/07/how-the-college-debt-is-crippling-students-parents-and-the-economy/.

Donahue, B. (2002). Anti-Muslim crimes jump after Sept. 11 in Jersey and U.S. In P.S. Rothenberg (ed.) *Race, Class and Gender in the United States*. New York, NY: Worth Publishers.

Eitzen, D.S., & Zinn, M.B. (1997). *Social Problems*. Needham Heights, MA: Allyn & Bacon.

Ferrante, J. (2008). *Sociology: A Global Perspective*. Belmont, CA: Thomson Higher Education.

Fukuyama, F. (1994). Immigrants and family values. In N. Mills (ed.) *Arguing Immigration*. New York, NY: Simon & Schuster.

Geertz, C. (1966). Religion as a cultural system. In M. Banton (ed.) *Anthropological Approaches to the Study of Religion*. London: Tavistock.

Ginther, D.K., & Hayes, K.J. (2003). Gender differences in salary and promotion for faculty in the humanities. *Journal of Human Resources, 38*(1), 34–73.

Ham, W. (1922). Harvard student opinion and the Jewish question. *The Journal of Education, 96*(11), 293–294.

Harris III, F., & Bensimon, E.M. (2007). The equity scorecard: A collaborative approach to assess and respond to racial/ethnic disparities in student outcomes. *New Directions for Student Services, 120*, 77–84.

Harvard University. (2015). Harvard at a glance. Retrieved from www.harvard.edu/harvard-glance.

Hossler, D., Schmit, J., & Vesper, N. (1999). *How Social, Economic, and Educational Factors Influence the Decisions Students Make*. Baltimore, MD: The Johns Hopkins University Press.

Johnson, L. (2012, October 25). Colin Powell endorses Obama. *Huffington Post*. Retrieved from www.huffingtonpost.com/2012/10/25/colin-powell-endorses-obama_n_2011162.html.

Kendall, D. (2000). *Sociology in our Times*. Belmont, CA: Wadsworth.

McBride, T. (2011). *The Mindset Lists of American History: From Typewriters to Text Messages, What Ten Generations of Americans Think Is Normal*. Hoboken, NJ: John Wiley & Sons.

McGuire, M.B. (1997). *Religion: The Social Context*. Belmont, CA: Wadsworth.

Munce, D. (2005, December 29). Achieving diversity on campus: A better approach. *Diverse Issues in Higher Education*. Retrieved from: http://diverseeducation.com/article/5263/.

Nora, A. (2004). The role of habitus and cultural capital in choosing a college, transitioning from high school to higher education, and persisting in college among minority and nonminority students. *Journal of Hispanic Higher Education*, 3(2), 180–208.

Nuguyen, T. (2005). *We Are All Suspects Now: Untold Stories from Immigrant Communities after 9/11*. Boston: MA: Beacon Press.

Pew Research Center. (2015). *U.S. Doesn't Rank High in Religious Diversity*. Retrieved from www.pewresearch.org/fact-tank/2014/04/04/u-s-doesnt-rank-high-in-religious-diversity/.

Postman, N. (1996). *The End of Education: Redefining the Value of School*. New York, NY: Vintage Books.

Rhone, N. (2006, May/June). How universities are keeping diversity on campus. *The Crisis, 113*(3), 10.

Schaefer, R.T. (2011). *Racial and Ethnic Groups*. Upper Saddle River, NJ: Saddle River Books.

Scott, J.W. (2007). *The Politics of the Veil*. Princeton, NJ: Princeton University Press.

Seifert, T. (2007). Understanding Christian privilege: Managing the tensions of spiritual plurality. *About Campus, 12*(2), 10–17.

Smith, R. (2013, October 13). Why Turkey lifted its ban on the Islamic headscarf. *National Geographic*. Retrieved from: http://news.nationalgeographic.com/news/2013/10/131011-hijab-ban-turkey-islamic-headscarf-ataturk/#.

Smith, T.W. (2002). Religious diversity in America: The emergence of Muslims, Buddhists, Hindus and Others. *Journal for the Scientific Study of Religion, 41*(3), 577–585.

Sowell, T. (1981). *Ethnic America: A History*. New York, NY: Basic Books.

Taylor, R.L. (2002). *Minority Families in the United States: A Multicultural Perspective*. Upper Saddle River, NJ: Prentiss Hall.

The University of Oregon. (2015). Retrieved from http://gladstone.uoregon.edu/~asuomca/diversityinit/definition.html.

Waggoner, M.D. (2011). *Sacred and Secular Tensions in Higher Education: Connecting Parallel Universities*. New York, NY: Taylor & Francis.

West, C. (2005). *Democracy Matters: Winning the Fight Against Imperialism*. New York, NY: Penguin Group.

Wilder, C.S. (2013). *Ebony and Ivy: Race, Slavery and the Troubled History of America's Universities*. New York: NY: Bloomsbury Press.

Woolbright, C. (1989). *Valuing Diversity on Campus: A Multicultural Approach*. Bloomington, IN: Association of College Unions-International.

Chapter 2

Existing Research on Religious Minorities on College Campuses

Starting college studies is a time of great transition in a student's life. The independence of being away from home can be so alluring that, even upon graduation, students may not choose to return home. In the same vein and despite its rewards, college can be a socially, financially, emotionally, and spiritually taxing experience (Cohen, 2013). If we view education as a type of work for the college student, then students who feel alienated may not be as self-actualized as their counterparts who may feel some sense of mastery (Knapp, 1994).

Furthermore, the college and university of today are often considered more secular than spiritual. It is unclear what role (if any) religion plays on American college campuses (Schmalzbauer, 2013). To top it off, evidence suggests that the American college student of today has increasingly grown more and more narcissistic (Twenge & Campbell, 2009). A strong sense of entitlement may lead students to say comments such as "It is necessary that I receive an A in this course," think they should get preferential treatment by a professor if they are making an effort in the course, feel as if they should receive a B just for showing up to class, or even be able to make up their final examination if it happens to affect their plan for the break (Twenge & Campbell, 2009). If college students are increasingly self-absorbed, how will they learn to act altruistically and be selfless instead of selfish?

PREVIOUS STUDIES OF RELIGION IN HIGHER EDUCATION

A major critique of previous studies of religion on college campuses is that they often fail to highlight the lived and discussed experiences of students who subscribe to some form of religion (Cherry, DeBerg, & Porterfield, 2001). Cherry and colleagues decided to conduct a case study of four geographically different American universities which sought to understand more deeply the religious practices, campus moral beliefs (ethos), and the teaching of religion on their respective campuses via interviews with undergraduates and campus personnel. The authors found the following in terms of religious practice:

> Influenced by the forces described by Wuthnow and Beaudoin, most of the undergraduates we encountered on the four campuses could be characterized as spiritual seekers rather than religious dwellers, and many of them were constructing their spirituality without much regard to the boundaries dividing religious denominations, traditions, or organizations.
>
> (pp. 276–277)

Research Regarding the Challenges Associated with Being a Religious Minority

Research has indicated that religious minorities may have various challenges navigating the collegiate experience. In an important study by Patten and Rice (2009), the academic perseverance of 1,879 freshman students was measured at a conservative, private, south central university in the United States. Results indicated that students who were not affiliated with the religious majority group (share institutional religious affiliation) were 11.2% less prone to continue their academic pursuits and enroll as a sophomore. Patten and Rice's study suggests that the experiences of religious majority and minority groups may affect college retention rates.

The current chapter will review existing books and articles on the experiences of religious minorities on college campuses. In accordance with the scholarly discussions of Bowman and Small (2010) and Swatos (1998), religious minorities include underrepresented religious minorities, including Jews, Muslims, Buddhists, Sikhs, Hindus, and other Christian religious minorities (Quakers, Mormons, and Unitarians) who are viewed to have theologically departed from traditional Christianity. For the purposes of brevity, the current chapter will focus on existing studies of Jewish, Muslim, Buddhist, Hindu and Animist college students.

ANIMIST, BUDDHIST, AND HINDU STUDENTS

Animism is a form of sacramental religion. Under animism, the idea of what is sacred "is sought in places, objects, and actions believed to house a god or spirit" (Ferrante, 2008). Thus animist religion is inextricably tied to nature. Traditional Native American indigenous religions fall under the umbrella of animism. Although different tribes have different religious mythologies, the tribal mythologies share similarities in terms of their views on the importance of connections not only among tribal members but also within the larger universe, which also comprises of plants and animals (Champagne, 1994).

Animism in College Students

A 1957 study by Crowell and Dole examined the link between animism, educational experiences, and college aptitude. Animism was measured by self-reported data on whether an array of objects were considered living or non-living. These objects ranged from something minute, such as an unlighted match, to something larger, such as the Earth. Out of a sample of 225 students at the University of Hawaii, animist thinking was found in 70% of the students. Results indicate a modest relationship between animist thinking and intelligence. One issue with this study is that it attempts to link self-reported animism with intellectual aptitude. Another study by Drywater-Whitekiller (2010) examined cultural resiliency among Native American college students using ten qualitative interviews. Patterns that emerged from the data suggested that both Christian and non-Christian Native American students prayed, with gratitude being an important theme among both groups. Of particular interest was the importance of displaying gratitude not only toward the Creator but toward the rain, the sun, motivation, education, intellectual and athletic aptitude, and assisting others. Perhaps students who practice animism or have animistic beliefs may have a beneficial impact for environmental justice movements based on their belief system.

Future studies that are conducted on or about religious minorities should avoid bias and subjectivity in favor of objectivity and fact-seeking. It would also be interesting if future studies examined the relationship between animism and environmental activism among college students. The belief that the Earth is a living object may mean that such students have an environmental consciousness that their non-animist counterparts may or may not subscribe to.

Based on the review of the existing literature, very little research exists on atheist, agnostic, or animist college students in the United States. Given the number of social science research studies that utilize college students as part of their samples, I suspect that, although such students are included in studies, they are not necessarily identified as atheist, animist, or agnostic. There is a growing debate that college campuses breed irreligious norms and values (see Calhoun, Aronczyk, Maryl, & VanAntwerpen, 2007). Future research is sorely needed on such groups to ensure that their needs are properly met on college campuses.

Buddhist Students

Buddhism is a spiritual path that focuses on inward reflection in order to be a true servant of humanity. It is based on the teachings of the Buddha, the namesake for the religion. Buddha grew up in a wealthy family where excess was the norm. He apparently indulged in everything at his disposal, including women and lavish items. It was not until he was older and ventured out of his fortified existence that he was able to see people who had been absolved of all material wealth. From this point onward, he was moved to live without the material pleasures that life had already afforded him. In the process, he was able to gain a deeper level of understanding of the human condition and the condition of his own self (Armstrong, 2004). Thus, major Buddhist teachings correspond to four noble truths, including: the truth of suffering, causes of suffering, ways to stop suffering and its causes, and the path to the cessation of suffering (Chodron, 2001).

Few studies have explored the experiences of Buddhist religious minorities on college campuses. One book by Storch (2015) examined how Buddhist teachings can serve as a model for higher education in the United States. She primarily focuses on four relatively unknown Buddhist-inspired universities in America, three of which are located in California and one in the state of Colorado. The universities mentioned in her book were as follows, in the order they were founded: 1) Naropa University, Boulder, Colorado (founded in 1974); 2) Dharma Realm University, City of Ten Thousand Buddhas, California (founded in 1976); 3) Soka University of America, Aliso Viejo, California (founded in 1987); and 4) The University of the West, Rosemead, California (founded in 1991).

Storch argues that Buddhist pedagogy may be the very solution to the crises in American higher education. She describes Buddhist pedagogy as one that is focused and beneficial in day-to-day life. The university is perceived as one community with shared goals and which operates as a family. The end result is to produce graduates who will be transformed as individuals but such universities seek to ameliorate local communities as well. Many may be skeptics of such an approach to education. However, data suggest that Buddhist university students not only graduate and work in their respective professions but many also continue on to graduate school. The oldest Buddhist University, Naropa University, has the following interesting undergraduate majors: Contemplative Psychology, Peace Studies, Religious Studies, Music, and Creative Writing and Literature, among others. Naropa also offers graduate degree programs in various areas. Naropa boasts small class sizes and a special curricular model entitled Contemplative Education. This model utilizes a three-prong approach to the education of students, including third-person inquiry, second-person inquiry, and first-person inquiry. All three approaches incorporate conventional academics with exploratory and contemplative learning to produce a more holistic curriculum (Naropa University, 2015).

Further research is desperately needed in terms of the on-campus experiences of Animist, Buddhist and Hindu religious minority students.

Hindu Students

Hinduism predates the Abrahamic faiths (Judaism, Christianity, and Islam) and has the rank of being considered among the world's oldest living religions still in practice. Hindus believe that living creatures, great and small, will be reincarnated (McKin, 2012). This reincarnation for human beings is a reflection of what acts (good or bad) were done during one's lifetime. Karma represents the law of return in that an individual will eventually reap what they sow.

Research Themes on Animist, Buddhist, and Hindu Students

1. Animist students: Previous studies of animist beliefs of American college students linked them to a lack of intelligence and thus were pejorative and biased. Other studies suggest that both Christian and non-Christian Native American students may have more similar worldviews than expected.
2. Buddhist students: Although no studies were found regarding Buddhist college students, it is refreshing to see the growth of Buddhist-inspired universities across America.
3. Unfortunately, there is limited research regarding the experiences of Hindu college students in America.

JEWISH STUDENTS

Judaism is considered to be the forerunner of scriptural monotheistic religion. Although being monotheistic was considered to be an honor among Jews and a representation of God's preference for them over other peoples, it was not necessarily accepted in the largely historically polytheistic world they entered into. Jewish history represents not only a past of struggle and persecution but also one of perseverance in the face of adversity. Today, Judaism is not considered to be a major world religion in terms of the number of followers, yet Judaism has had a definite influence on the religions of Christianity and Islam, the world's first and second largest religions, respectively.

Among religious minority students, Jewish students have historically faced high levels of anti-Semitism in American educational institutions. This was largely due to the fact that they were one of the first European immigrant groups who went to college in large numbers and were considered to be among the lowest European races among the Protestant elite. Quotas limiting the admission of Jews and speech tests were used to prevent educational mobility (Brodkin, 2002). It was not until 2010 that the civil rights protections outlined in the 1964 Civil Rights Act were extended by the Department of Education to include persons who were the recipients of anti-religious bias.

Studies of Jewish Students at American Universities

A mid-century study of 180 Jewish freshman students at the University of Maryland by Greenberg (1961) yielded demographic and social background information of the Jewish student participants. Jewish students were found to be third-generation Jewish Americans whose grandparents primarily immigrated from the Eastern European countries of Russia, Poland, and Romania. The majority of students came from Baltimore and Washington, D.C., which is historically suggestive of the flight out of these same cities decades later often entitled "white flight." Most of the students' parents were business proprietors or professionals and thus financially able to send their children to college. There also seemed to be a Jewish family influence on the importance of education as a pathway toward upward mobility. As such, most of the parents were considered middle class. Of an interesting note was that most of the students' grandparents immigrated to the United States during a nine-year window (1900–1909) due to highly restrictive U.S. immigration policies. This is evidence of American abhorrence toward persons of the Jewish faith. Exclusionary immigration policies limited perceived competition between Jews and Americans. Most students came from two-child families where Yiddish was spoken in the home occasionally or regularly.

In a 1965 study of contact, compliance and distance among Jewish and non-Jewish undergraduates by Segal, a systematic sample of 100 Jewish and 105 non-Jewish students was taken at a four-year college for men in the Northeast. Jewish students were approximately one-sixth of the student body, with a total enrollment of 3,000 students. Social distance was measured by a five-point Likert scale where students were asked to indicate the degree to which they would like to engage with Jews or non-Jews in various social situations. Results indicated that Jews were less likely to be socially distant than their non-Jewish counterparts. Jewish students also tended to have more non-Jewish than Jewish friends. Probably one of the more interesting components to the study was that each group estimated the social distance of the other. More specifically, each group was requested to respond as if they were a member of the other group. Both groups tended to overestimate the other group's social distance. In other words, each group thought the other group would be more socially distant than they were in reality.

The results of this study shed light on the fact that religious minorities may be more willing to engage with dominant majority groups than vice versa. It also suggests that students in the dominant group may not go out of their way to engage with students outside of their social circles. One of the critiques of the study was that the authors did not explicitly mention the social situations which may lead to social contact among the two groups, making replication a major issue. Lastly, since the campus environment was already primarily non-Jewish, it was unclear if Jews only appeared to be less socially distant due to lower possibilities of coming into contact with other Jews, as opposed to a desire to have contact with the opposite (non-Jewish) group.

There is surprisingly very scant information on Jewish college students, despite their long-running history with institutions of higher education. It was refreshing to find a qualitative study about the Shabbos experience on five different campuses (Chazan & Bryfman, 2006). The Chabad-Lubavitch movement opened over 85 houses on or near college campuses containing large Jewish populations over a five-year period. The houses are sponsored through the donations of largely unorthodox sponsors. Special Shabbat meals are given on a weekly basis, which may attract large numbers of Jewish graduate and undergraduate students. Although these dinners are traditional and employ Jewish religious rituals, they are open to orthodox/non-orthodox Jews alike.

Jewish students who went to the Shabbat dinners were interviewed in regards to their Shabbos experiences. On a positive note, it was found that many Jewish student participants found the houses to be a "home away from home" and a type of fictive family of sorts, which led them to return on several occasions. Other themes that emerged were the centrality of food in the lives of the students, the acceptance of religious rituals associated with the Shabbos (e.g., donning a yarmulke, candle lighting, recitation of blessings after the meal), and the listening of the rabbi or wife's religious teachings at the time of the dinner. However, some students did indicate that there was definitely an agenda involved with the experience and that they felt pressure to conform to traditional Jewish standards and exhibit a greater degree of Jewish practice while in attendance at the dinner.

Given the limited number of articles related to Jewish American college students, refuge in the book arena was sought out. Two books published in 2010 were found on a similar topic, and attempt to satisfy the dearth in the literature by providing information on how to navigate the college experience as a Jewish student. Both books attempt to examine the realities associated with being a Jewish student while most likely attending a primarily secular institution.

Jewish University: A Contemporary Guide for the College Student explores an array of relevant topics related to college life. The topics included the following: negotiating leaving home and packing for school, which I will entitle 'pre-college preparatory activities'; college arrival activities, such as life in the dorm, roommates, and diet; and more serious topics such as how to handle religious holidays away from home, Passover on campus, Shavuot all-nighters, how to relate to persons of different backgrounds, and even sexual decision-making (Aaron, 2010).

The other, related book, by David Schoem (2010), offers over 100 tips for Jewish college students as they navigate the college experience. For the purposes of brevity, some of the more central tips will be shared below. Schoem offers general tips on how to be a successful college student, making the best out of one's college experience (e.g., learning Hebrew if available), being a good student and taking one's studies seriously, the development of a social justice commitment, the importance of mispatcha (family), finances, practicing safe sex, limited alcohol use and drug avoidance, the exploration of one's campus and local Jewish community, and learning from one's religious minority experience.

Anti-Semitism

In an attempt to clarify what exactly constitutes anti-Semitism on campus, a letter was written by the American Association of University Professors and American Jewish Committee. They suggest that anti-Semitism cannot be misconstrued with anti-Israeli sentiment on a college or university campus as this would be a violation of freedom of speech. According to Douglas Giles (2011), his academic freedom as well as that of his students was violated when he was discouraged to discuss Zionism and Muslim and Jewish beliefs about the Holy Land in his class.

Rather, they suggest that a working definition of anti-Semitism would generally include the following: suggesting that Jews do not have the right to self-determination and that Zionism equates to racism, blaming the collective lot of Jews for the actions of the Israeli state, and linking Israeli policy to that of the Nazis (American Association of University Professors & American Jewish Committee, 2011). Claims of anti-Semitism should be taken very seriously by university officials and it is the role of the university to attempt to ensure that colleges are free from harassment and intimidation based on religious preferences. Guest lectures from scholars in the field, classes which discuss the roots of animosity, and surveying students about their personal experiences with bigotry are among the few recommendations for potential anti-Semitism on campus (American Association of University Professors & American Jewish Committee, 2011).

Research Themes of Studies on Jewish Students

1. Studies compare and contrast Jews with a standard or more "normalized" group such as Christians or non-Jewish students.
2. There are challenges associated with assimilation or losing one's ethnic and religious identity in college.
3. There are studies which encourage Jews to forge their own path, whether it is a religious one or not.

MUSLIM STUDENTS

Islam is the world's fastest growing religion and the second largest religion in the world, despite its more recent inception over 1,400 years ago. The quintessential element of Islam is the belief in complete monotheism; in other words, one omnipotent creator without partners or offspring who is responsible for the existence of everything that has existed, presently exists, and will exist in the future. The remaining features of Islam include salat, or prayer, performed five times daily; zakat, the giving of 2.5% of one's wealth; fasting from pre-dawn to sunset during the holy month of Ramadan; and Hajj, or pilgrimage, to Makkah. From the outside looking in, Islam may appear highly ritualistic. However, to the practicing Muslim, they may find their practices deeply introspective. Books such as *Purification of the Heart* by Muslim American scholar Hamza Yusuf, Yasmin Mogahed's *Reclaim Your Heart* and works by the late Islamic scholar Imam Al-Ghazali underscore and highlight the importance of struggling against one's own self in order to prevent one's downfall (Yusuf, 2012; Mogahed, 2012; see Al-Ghazali, 2014).

Based on a perusal of the literature, it is interesting to note that many of the research studies published regarding Muslim college students have been published after September 11, 2001. After 9/11, there was both a surge and a shift in research which sought to understand the attitudes and experiences of Muslims. Although Muslims have been part of America for centuries (Diouf, 1998; GhaneaBassiri, 2010; Manseau, 2015), 9/11 served to put Islam under the spotlight, albeit a negative one. As such, this event most likely had a profound effect on Muslim students since, at the time, the American public knew very little about Islam. Despite 9/11 being 15 years ago, it seems that it will forever follow Muslims like a dark rain cloud that may not always produce a downpour but will never go away in the American psyche. Of course it must be dismantled that serious academic discussions of Muslims in higher education have only taken place in a post-9/11 context.

The article by Nasir and Al-Amin (2006) provides valuable insight into the challenges associated with being Muslim on campus. The authors conducted several interviews of Muslim college students but chose to focus on the stories of two in particular, Rashid and Fatima. Rashid is an African-American convert to Islam who went to college on an athletic scholarship. Rashid encountered major challenges following his conversion to Islam in the sophomore year of college. Despite having a previously good relationship with his coach, after his conversion, his coach accused him of being a Black nationalist and radical, and later told him he should not come back to the team the following season. Rashid also found himself having an ideological struggle with the lectures of an Islamic Studies professor who was not Muslim. Rashid felt this particular professor painted Islam in a very negative light and assigned readings to prove his bias toward Islam. Rashid later dropped out of school a few credits shy of graduation, only to return a few years later to finally complete his degree. Fatima, on the other hand, was from a well-to-do Pakistani-headed family. She made the conscious decision to wear hijab on campus. After the fact, she felt that she was still treated well and even encouraged to continue to cover through positive affirmations from outside sources (i.e., her professor) (Nasir & Al-Amin, 2006).

Many of the Muslim students interviewed struggled with managing the impressions that persons who were not Muslim had of them. Thus, they were overly self-conscious of themselves and their potential actions. For example, Fatima struggled with her appearance after she started wearing the hijab since she did not want to look like a "foreigner." She also expressed challenges associated with making ritual ablution and finding a proper location/space to make prayer. Acts of kindness (even if small) were found to have the most positive effect on the experiences of the Muslim students. For instance, after wearing the hijab, Fatima's professor commented on how pretty she looked wearing it. This act of kindness potentially strengthened Fatima's resolve to continue to cover despite her insecurities as to how she would be perceived (Nasir & Al-Amin, 2006).

Furthermore, the authors suggested that for religious minority students such as Muslims, their student experiences are shaped by the following (Figure 2.1):

1. Student characteristics (e.g., race, gender, ethnicity, religion, age).
2. Campus characteristics (liberal, conservative, small/large student body, religious affiliation of school, presence or absence of Muslim faculty, Muslim Students Association).
3. Surrounding community characteristics (liberal, conservative, rural, urban, Muslim presence).

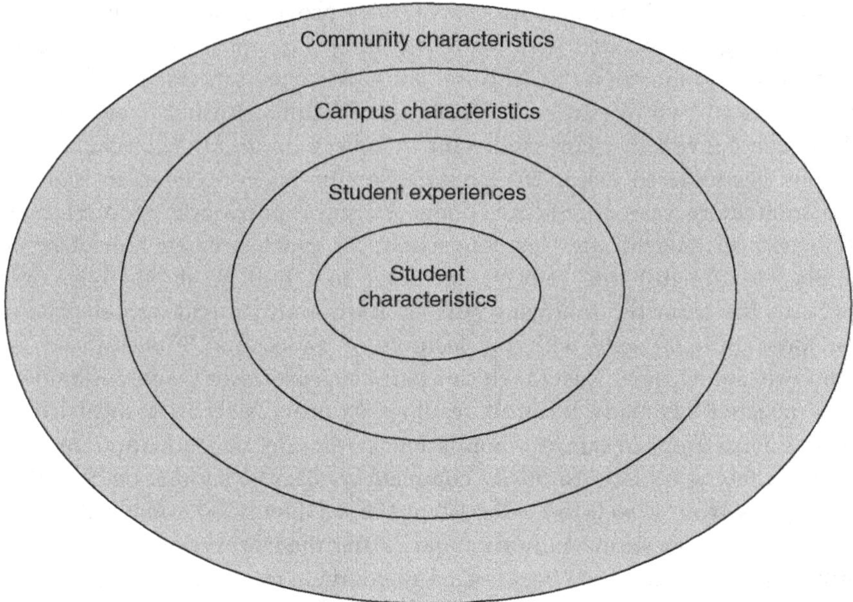

Figure 2.1 Factors Affecting Muslim Students' Experiences

Another central study by Cole and Ahmadi (2010) highlighted the experiences of Muslim college students in comparison to both Jewish and Christian students. Students were measured at two time points: their freshman and senior years. The total sample size consisted of 203 students, with 66 Muslim students, 67 Jewish, and 70 Christian students. Muslim students in the sample were more likely to speak English as a second or third language, were older, were less likely to be U.S. citizens, and were more racially and ethnically diverse than their Christian and Jewish counterparts. The majority of the students came from universities which were private, four-year institutions. The goal of the study was to understand how Muslim self-identification shapes one's college experiences. Furthermore, religious differences in educational achievement may lead to a decreased level of academic satisfaction on the part of the study participants.

The college experience was operationalized by the following variables: religion, interracial interactions, peer involvement in academic activities, and student/faculty interaction. For the fourth year only, average college grade and overall satisfaction with the college experiences was measured. Of the 15 college experience variables, eight of the 15 indicated statistically significant differences using ANOVA. The result suggested that Muslim students were more likely to tutor another student, attend racial/cultural awareness workshops, have a roommate of a different racial/ethnic background, socialize with different ethnic groups, and "participate" in racial/ethnic specific organizations. In contrast, Muslim students spent less time in religious service/prayer than their counterparts. Overall, Muslim students were less satisfied with their overall college experience than their Jewish counterparts.

Challenges Associated with Being a Muslim Female College Student

According to Ali and Bagheri (2009), Muslim students may be alienated on college campuses due to being a religious minority. The rising tide of Islamophobia post 9/11 may cause Muslim students and students of other faith backgrounds (e.g., Hindu students who wear turbans) to feel less secure and safe to openly practice their religion. The authors offer suggestions to improve the quality of life for Muslim students on campus. Ali and Bagheri also suggest that Muslim female students, in particular, may need greater institutional support since they visibly cover and may be subject to more questions/criticism as a result of their physical appearance. There seemed to be a common theme among the studies on Muslim students regarding the experiences of Muslim female college students. Two studies in particular shed light on the plight of Muslim women on college campuses post 9/11 (Williams & Vashi, 2007; Maruoka, 2008).

In terms of the Williams and Vashi study, data were collected through focus group interviews and individual interviews of 40 Muslim women (18–25), 75% of whom were in college. The primary goal of the study was to understand the role of the hijab for American Muslim women. Findings revealed that the hijab serves several varying functions for the women in the study based on their interview data. The hijab primarily serves as a religious symbol that one belongs to the Muslim faith, self-identifies as a Muslim, and may be identified as a Muslim by others. It also may be used to dress more modestly through the covering of the hair and the bosom. As such, it was revealed that not wearing the hijab may be potentially isolating for some Muslim women who choose not to do so in the campus community. Another interesting finding that came out of the research was that the hijab may be used as a form of resistance. Some women wore hijab in opposition to the home practices of their Muslim parent's wishes. Lastly, the hijab also functions as a fashion statement. Muslim college students commented on each other's hijabs in terms of color, drape, design, and overall appearance. These findings suggest that the hijab has different meanings for Muslim women. It would be interesting to see a study which also explores how persons who are not Muslim view the hijab and if their definition of it varies as much as Muslim college students.

In 2014, a poignant book was published by Shabana Mir entitled *Muslim American Women on Campus: Undergraduate Social Life and Identity*. It is refreshing to find the research of Muslim females coming to the forefront in terms of religious diversity in higher education. As stated previously, a common re-occurring theme among several of the studies on Muslim college students was to further understand Muslim women's experiences. One of the common stereotypes about Muslim women is that they are oppressed. In the context of Muslim female college students in America, it appears that campus micro aggressions post 9/11 were much more dangerous than the Muslim faith the students practiced.

For the study by Maruoka (2008), data were primarily obtained through participant observation of 100 Muslim Student Association activities, as well as 40 in-depth interviews of second-generation South Asian Muslim female college students from two different universities in the state of New York. The study's goal was to examine South Asian Muslim women's student activism in a post 9/11 context. The cases of Habiba and Zayda were very alarming to read but need to be discussed. According to Habiba:

> After September 11, there were a lot of things that happened around us. The news said that some people tried to take off Muslim women's scarves and run them over with their cars. On campus, some guys tried to threaten us in the same way. They chased after my friend and me, and tried to take off our scarves from their car. It happened more than once.
>
> (Maruoka, 2008, p. 122)

Zayda shared a similar alarming story after 9/11 had just happened:

> One of the brothers told me that he and his roommate overheard, while in a laundry room in their dorm, that some guys were talking to each other like, "This Saturday night, Sunday night, or some other party night, we're gonna go out, rip those girls' scarves off, rip their clothes off, and rape them…" It was a scary time…. We really got scared. So, we just stayed in our room and locked ourselves in.
>
> (Maruoka, 2008, p. 122)

As many as 35 of the 40 female Muslim students expressed some form of anxiety regarding wearing the hijab after 9/11. Muslim female college students also reported to consistently hear the phrase "Go back to your country!", which is consistent with xenophobic ideologies which promote intolerance, hatred, and disgust for groups perceived to be of immigrant origin.

This study indicates the ignorance of students who make threats which are sometimes empty and sometimes acted upon. It suggests that xenophobia may have a much firmer grasp and reach outside of the classroom where it may be considered more permissible for students to be with peer groups and feel comfortable saying or doing bad behavior. Perhaps there is a lack of fear of reprisal, to act out their impulses outside of the classroom, and a greater sense of anonymity. The study also illustrates student passivity as many onlookers did not address or even speak out against such negative occurrences. For instance, Sara stated,

> When my friend and I were walking on campus after September 11, some guys yelled at us, like "take off your scarf!" And a couple of them followed right behind us. The other people looked at us and, well, all pretty much giggling.
>
> (Maruoka, 2008, p. 122)

Individual-level racism will continue to thrive if student passivity is left unchecked. The act of doing or saying nothing while witnessing racism or discrimination is a passive and informal way of supporting such acts (Katz, 1989). Studies suggest that participation in interfaith work and cooperation may serve to break down the largely self-imposed barriers between persons of different faith backgrounds (Stedman, 2011).

Campus environments should have a zero-tolerance policy for harassment (physical, verbal, or otherwise). This policy must not only be reiterated to ensure students understand but also implemented so that students understand its severity. In order to resist the negative post 9/11 atmosphere on campus, Muslim women students participated in a variety of campus outreach activities. Most notably, Muslim female students reached out to other communities in the wake of 9/11 to avoid becoming insular and to open up dialogue. The students also promoted unity among the members of the Muslim Student Association. Lastly, Muslim female students wanted to show that Muslim women who wore hijab also had depth to them in their education efforts and are just normal people who just happen to cover their hair (Maruoka, 2008).

Muslim college students may be eager to go to a school where they are more likely to find other Muslim college students and organizations. This may particularly hold true for students that have a strong religious identity or may feel stigmatized in some way as being an outsider. Tarek Elgawhary, a junior religion major at George Washington University, stated that his decision to go to GWU was because he felt it would be an environment that would be conducive to his Muslim faith. The university boasts over 1,000 Muslim students and therefore they may have more resources at their disposal for Tarek to thrive with (Beliefnet, 2015).

Research Themes in the Literature on Muslim College Students

1. The majority of the studies take place in a post-9/11 context.
2. Many of the studies focus on issues pertaining to Muslim women and their subsequent experiences.
3. There is a focus on challenges associated with practicing one's Muslim faith on a college campus.

SUMMATION OF THE LITERATURE

In conclusion, there are virtually no studies that examine the experiences of agnostic, atheist, animist, Buddhist, Sikh, or Hindu college students in the United States. Those religious minority groups with the most research have been Jewish and Muslim religious minority students. However, the studies of Muslim college students is more diverse, based on topic, and more recent, with the majority of studies appearing after September 11, 2001. Those studies on Jewish college students are few in nature given that Jewish religious minority students have accessed higher education longer than any other religious minority group.

Table 2.1 highlights some of the areas of concern for religious minorities in higher education as well as potential solutions.

Table 2.2 shows the prayer and multifaith prayer spaces at selected college campuses across the United States as advertised on university/college websites. These universities in particular most probably want to be seen as institutions that cater to students of diverse faith backgrounds. Many other universities may have prayer spaces on campus for religious minorities but may not see it prudent to advertise them on their website for potential students.

MULTIFAITH/INTERFAITH INITIATIVES

University and college campuses are excellent places to hold interfaith and multifaith, multi-racial initiatives which promote dialogue not only between students, faculty, and staff on campus, but also members of the larger local community (Winkle-Wagner & Locks, 2013). Colleges and university students, despite their differences, have many commonalities and share the common ground of humanity, which should always be remembered. The Golden Rule is often translated as "Do to others as you want others to do to you," but many persons miss the true wisdom behind this rule. According to Wattles (1996), the rule has merit for the religious and irreligious alike and provides a strong foundation for human social interaction.

Table 2.1 Challenges for Religious Minorities in Higher Education and
Potential Solutions

Religious Minority	Challenges	Potential Solutions
Animists	Eurocentric curriculum School calendar which may conflict with Animist holidays	Multicultural curriculum Animist holidays on the school calendar
Buddhists	Eurocentric curriculum Lack of meditation space on campus	Multicultural curriculum Meditation room
Hindus	Eurocentric curriculum Dietary restrictions School calendar which may conflict with Hindu holidays Threats/harassment/student intimidation	Multicultural curriculum Expanded vegetarian options
Jews	Eurocentric curriculum (Christian-centered) Dietary restrictions School calendar which may conflict with Jewish holidays	Multicultural curriculum Expanded kosher options
Muslims	Eurocentric curriculum Dietary limits (no pork, alcohol) School calendar which may conflict with Muslim holidays Lack of a physical prayer space on campus Classes which conflict with prayer times Threats/harassment/student intimidation	Multicultural curriculum Expanded kosher/zabiha options Muslim prayer room or rooms on campus or an interfaith prayer/reflection room on campus

The following scriptural quotes may be used to support interfaith discussion on college campuses:

And if a man from another country is living in your land with you, do not make life hard for him; Let him be to you as one of your countrymen and have love for him as for yourself; for you were living in a strange land, in the land of Egypt: I am the Yehovah your God.

(Leviticus, 19:33–34)

There are doubtless many different languages in the world, and none is without meaning....

(Corinthians 14:10)

O mankind! We created you from a single (pair) of a male and a female, and made you into nations and tribes, that ye may know each other not that ye may despise (each other). Verily the most honoured of you in the

Table 2.2 Prayer Rooms Advertised on University/College Websites

	School	Religious Accommodation
1.	University of Portland	Muslim prayer room
2.	Grove City College	General prayer room
3.	University of Southern California	Muslim prayer room
4.	Rutgers University	Interfaith prayer room
5.	Stanford University	Muslim prayer room
6.	University of Pennsylvania	Muslim Students Association prayer room
7.	Missouri University	Several campus prayer locations
8.	Marygrove College	Muslim prayer room
9.	Georgetown University	Muslim prayer room
10.	Columbia University	Prayer rooms, female-only prayer room
11.	University of Michigan	Reflection rooms, chapel (allows for different faiths to pray inside)
12.	Northwestern University	Prayer rooms, meditation rooms
13.	Marquette University	Islamic prayer room
14.	Merrimack College	Common prayer room
15.	American University	Kay Spiritual Life Center, Muslim prayer room
16.	University of Notre Dame	Meditation room
17.	North Carolina State University	Interfaith prayer and meditation space
18.	Oberlin College	Muslim prayer room
19.	Regent University	Chapel, small prayer room
20.	Tufts University	Chapel, Hillel Center, Interfaith Center
21.	Hofstra University	Interfaith Center
22.	Marist College	Chapel, Jewish services
23.	George Mason University	Campus ministries
24.	Seattle University	Multifaith prayer room
25.	University of Wisconsin, River Falls	Meditation room

Sources: University of Portland: www.up.edu/campusministry/default.aspx?cid=10760&pid=68; Grove City College: www.gcc.edu/about/Chapel/Campus-Ministries/Pages/Prayer-Rooms.aspx; University of Southern California: http://uscmuslims.com/campus/prayer-room; Rutgers: www.dailytargum.com/article/2013/09/rutgers-allots-space-for-interfaith-prayer-rooms; Stanford University: http://web.stanford.edu/group/ISSU/cgi-bin/wordpress/resources/prayer-room/; University of Pennsylvania: www.upennmsa.org/where-to-pray-on-campus/; Missouri University: www.mizzoumso.org/prayer-locations-on-campus.html; Marygrove college: www.cardinal newmansociety.org/CatholicEducationDaily/DetailsPage/tabid/102/ArticleID/2897/Marygrove-College-Adds-Muslim-Prayer-Room-to-Campus.aspx; Georgetown University: http://campusministry.georgetown.edu/about/sacredspaces/muslim_prayer/; Columbia University: http://columbiamsa.org/resources/praying/; University of Michigan: http://muslims.studentorgs.umich.edu/resources/prayer-information; Northwestern University: http://groups.northwestern.edu/mcsa/?page_id=61; Marquette University: www.marquette.edu/cm/worship/islamic-prayer-room.shtml; Merrimack College: www.merrimack.edu/live/news/1986-college-dedicates-new-space-for-prayer-by-those-of; American University: www.american.edu/ocl/kay/Worship-Schedule.cfm; University of Notre Dame: http://campusministry.nd.edu/undergraduate-resources/multicultural-resources/prayer-opportunities/; North Carolina State University: http://oied.ncsu.edu/diversity/interfaith-prayer-meditation-space/; Oberlin College: https://new.oberlin.edu/office/religious-and-spiritual-life/communities/; Regent University: https://www.regent.edu/about_us/campuses/campusmapflyer.pdf; Tufts University: http://chaplaincy.tufts.edu/on-campus-sacred-spaces/; Hofstra University: www.hofstra.edu/studentaffairs/studentservices/stsv_chaplains.html#panel4; Marist College: www.marist.edu/studentlife/ministry/activities_detail.html; George Mason University: http://mason.gmu.edu/~ministry/; Seattle University: www.seattleu.edu/campus-ministry/worship/sacred-spaces/; University of Wisconsin, River Falls: www.uwrf.edu/StudentHealthAndCounseling/CounselingServices/Meditation-Room.cfm.

sight of God is (he who is) the most righteous of you. And God has full knowledge and is well acquainted (with all things).

(Holy Qur'an, Surah Hujurat, 49:13)

Value knowledge over practice, meditation over knowledge; highest is renunciation, whence comes, immediately peace. Who does not hate any being, is friendly and compassionate, without possessiveness and ego, the same in grief and joy, enduring, the yogi who lives in content, firmly resolved and self-restrained, whose higher mind is fixed on me, who is devout is dear to me.

(The Bhagavad Gita 12:12–14; Flood, 2015)

In Cornel West's *Democracy Matters*, he uses the critically acclaimed author Toni Morrison as an insight into the importance of democracy. He states:

Morrison's fundamental insight is that there can be democratic dialogue only when one is open to the humanity of individuals and to the interiority of their personalities. Like the blues, Morrison assumes the full-fledged humanity of black people – a revolutionary gesture in a racist civilization – and thereby dethrones the superior status of whites. This assumption liberates both blacks and whites and enables them to embark on a candid, though painful, engagement with life and death, joy and sorrow, resistance and domination, hope and despair in the American empire.

(West, 2005, p. 100)

RECENT EVENTS

Recent events surrounding bigotry and hatred suggest that there is still a lot of room for growth in terms of cultural diversity and tolerance initiatives. On February 10, 2015, three Muslim students were killed by their estranged neighbor in their off-campus apartment near the campus of UNC Chapel Hill. One student (Mr. Deah Barakat) was a dental student at UNC Chapel Hill; his wife (Mrs. Yusor Abu-Salah) was supposed to start dental school in the fall. Yusor's sister, Razan, an undergraduate student at North Carolina State University, was also murdered. In response to the atrocious murders, the University of North Carolina at Chapel Hill held a press conference, prayer service, and vigil the day following the murders. The chancellors of UNC-Chapel Hill, North Carolina State University, and North Carolina Central University, the vice president of student affairs at Duke University, mayor of the town of Chapel Hill, the dean of UNC School of Dentistry, and the imam/chief representative of Muslim affairs were in attendance at the press conferences (University of North Carolina at Chapel Hill, 2015).

The prayer service and vigil were interfaith, which is suggestive of the agreement that such egregious acts should not be tolerated.

In other related news, on April 1, 2015, a noose was hung from a tree on the campus of Duke University. This drew a response of outrage from the campus community and students of color in particular. The noose was apparently found hanging on a tree that was close to the Duke University chapel. Protests ensued and Larry Moneta, vice president of student affairs, issued the following statement in response to the incident:

> All I want to say to our black students is that I love you all and black lives matter. I want to say to our Muslim students that Muslim lives matter. I want to say to our Christian students, to our Hindu students, to our Buddhist students, to our atheist students, all lives matter.
>
> (Almasy, 2015)

It is important to note that, in both incidents, the universities and colleges involved took swift action and issued statements that suggested that there was no room for hatred and bias on their respective campuses. Perhaps universities wish to maintain a public persona that their campuses are tolerant as opposed to xenophobic locations.

Tables 2.3 and 2.4 highlight tips for promoting peace and multicultural student services on college campuses.

Chapter 3 will discuss methods for campus climate assessment, such as surveys and focus groups. In particular, this chapter will discuss the appropriateness of various assessment methods for different campus types and needs. For example, a public institution in an urban area with a large commuter population will have different needs than a religiously affiliated college in a rural area with a primarily residential population.

DISCUSSION QUESTIONS

1. How might college life represent an amalgam of experiences?
2. What are some of the major challenges that religious minorities face in college?
3. Why do you imagine so little research exists about Animist, Buddhist, and Hindu college students in America? What does this suggest about the bias in the research of religious minorities?
4. In what ways may the challenges of Jewish and Muslim students be similar? In what ways may they be different?
5. How might it be difficult to decipher what is and what is not representative of anti-Semitism in the context of freedom of speech on campus?

Table 2.3 30 Tips Toward Building a Culture of Peace on College Campuses

See Conflict as Opportunity	Listen with Empathy	Commit to a Win-Win Solution	Honor Diversity	Practice Shared Responsibility
Have a Process for Conflict Resolution	Dialogue to Understand	Seek Common Ground and Consensus	Address Needs and Interests rather than Positions	Get Help from Third Parties
Turn Enemies into Allies	Build Bridges and Alliances	Refuse to Support an Adversarial Approach	Celebrate the Differences	Go Beyond Stereotypes and Prejudices
Practice Cross-Cultural Communication	See Yourself as the Other	Engage in Honest Conversation	Speak the Truth of your Experience	Acknowledge the Hurt
Apologize	Forgive	Right the Wrongs	Look at Historical Patterns	Inform Yourself
Take a Personal Privilege Inventory	Take an Interest in World Affairs	See Work as Service	Encourage Nonviolent Solutions to Conflict	Be a Voice for the Voiceless

Source: Tips were adapted from Diamond (2001).

Table 2.4 Best Practices in Multicultural Student Services at Various Colleges and Universities

Private Liberal Arts Colleges	Public Institutions	Community Colleges	Minority-Serving Institutions (HBCUs)	Minority-Serving Institutions (Tribal Colleges)
Engaging liberal arts curriculum	Multicultural student services should have high visibility on campus and are not geographically isolated	Enrollment of non-traditional students from various socio-economic backgrounds	Strong liberal arts curriculum	Core courses on tribal history and languages so students can have a direct impact on their communities
Creation of offices to support students of color devoted to multicultural student services	Cultivate students who are global citizens	Remediation courses for incoming students	Inclusive to students of various racial and socio-economic backgrounds	Required service learning courses
Faculty who propose new curriculum	Diverse student body	Culturally diverse student affairs personnel dedicated to expanding the quality of student life	Institutional culture which promotes multiculturalism	Community outreach programs designed to educate teachers and tribal leaders on various topics, e.g., science education
Core curriculum requirement which includes diversity	Regular campus climate assessments using multicultural audits	Multicultural student leadership programs giving students paid internships to serve as campus leaders	Focus on the within-group diversity of African Americans and those persons of African descent	Use of the family integration model to incorporate the family and extended family members of students into campus activities and events

Importance of academic deans being the leaders in diversity discussions	Support the retention of students from underrepresented groups	Provision of pre-enrollment and financial advice, assistance with financial aid applications	Consortium membership which allows for students to take courses elsewhere for credit	Day care facility for students who are also parents
Sponsoring of cultural celebrations	Increased course offerings that focus on issues of diversity and inclusion	International student activities, study abroad, and global studies	Religious services which are interdenominational ex. Martin Luther King Jr. International Chapel	Tribal elders used as mentors for students on campus
Academic enhancement services	New hires who are "multiculturally competent educators"	Provision of university materials which are not just limited to English	Students from different faith backgrounds may serve as chapel assistants	Hiring of full-time retention officer staff positions
Campus Cultural Houses	Create partnerships with off-campus religious organizations to promote religious tolerance on campus	TRIO Student Support Services federal grants to assist first-generation college students with economic hardship or disabilities	Cultural programming created by the students	Programs for tribal elders free of charge with the fulfillment of 64 credit hours (e.g., Honorary degree for Elders (HDE))
Offices of institutional equity and diversity	Inclusive programming and availability of "safe spaces" on campus	"StudentPal" program-tracking program to retain and provide directed programs for students of color	Incentive for high-performing students, e.g., Spring Tour-international trip for a week at no cost to the students to gain global awareness	Talking circle groups to further understand the barriers to male drop-out

Sources: Ferguson and Thomas-Rashid (2011). McCoy (2011). Zamani-Gallaher and Bazile (2011). Rome (2011). Riding In and Longwell-Grice (2011).

6. How have Muslim college students responded to the challenges they have faced post 9/11 in both positive and negative ways?
7. Should all campuses have multifaith/interfaith initiatives? Why or why not?
8. The recent events of hate and prejudice in North Carolina indicate that the college campus of today is not immune to such issues. What can and should be done on college campuses to promote peace and tolerance?
9. What can ordinary college students do when they directly hear or see racial/ethnic discriminatory injustices perpetrated by other students?
10. Go to the New York Times website (www.nyt.com). Type the following search terms in the search engine separately: Animism, Buddhism, Hinduism, Judaism, and Islam. What relevant headlines appear for each religion? Does this suggest anything about the way the media shapes our conceptions surrounding various religions?
11. Take the U.S. religious knowledge quiz (www.pewforum.org/2010/09/28/u-s-religious-knowledge-survey/) and compare your results to the rest of those surveyed. Write a short one-page critical summary of your results from the quiz and be prepared to share your findings with the class.

REFERENCES

Aaron, S. (2010). *Jewish University: A Contemporary Guide for the College Student*. New York, NY: URJ Press.

Al-Ghazali, I. (2014). *Mukhtasar: Ihya Ulum Ad-din*. Cyprus: Spohr Publishers.

Ali, S.R., & Bagheri, E. (2009). Practical suggestions to accommodate the needs of Muslim students on campus. *New Directions for Student Services, 125*, 47–54.

Almasy, S. (2015, April 3). Duke University: Student takes responsibility for noose found hanging on campus. *Cable News Network*. Retrieved from www.cnn.com/2015/04/02/us/north-carolina-duke-noose/index.html.

American Association of University Professors and American Jewish Committee. (2011). Anti-Semitism on campus. *Journal of Palestine Studies, 40*(4), 219–220.

Armstrong, K. (2004). *Buddha*. New York, NY: Penguin Books.

Beliefnet. (2015). College adapting to increased Muslim presence among students. Retrieved from www.beliefnet.com/Faiths/2000/03/Colleges-Adapting-To-Increased-Muslim-Presence-Among-Students.aspx?p=4.

Bowman, N.A., & Small, J.L. (2010). Do college students who identify with a privileged religion experience greater spiritual development? Exploring individual and institutional dynamics. *Research in Higher Education, 51*: 595–614.

Brodkin, K. (2002). How Jews became white folks and what that says about race in America. In P.S. Rothenberg (ed.) *Race, Class, and Gender in the United States*. New York, NY: Worth Publishers.

Calhoun, C., Aronczyk, M., Maryl, D., & VanAntwerpen, J. (2007). *Report Card: "A" for Atheist? The Religious Engagements of American Undergraduates*. New York, NY: Social Science Research Council.

Champagne, D. (1994). *Native America: Portrait of the Peoples*. Detroit, MI: Visible Ink Press.

Chazan, B., & Bryfman, D. (2006). *Home Away from Home: A Research Study of the Shabbos Experience on Five University Campuses: An Informal Educational Model for Working with Young Jewish Adults*. New York, NY: Chabad on Campus International Foundation.

Cherry, C., DeBerg, B.A., & Porterfield, A. (2001). *Religion on Campus: What Religion Really Means to Today's Undergraduates*. Chapel Hill, NC: University of North Carolina Press.

Chodron, T. (2001). *Buddhism for Beginners*. Boston, MA: Shambhala Publications Inc.

Cohen, H. (2013). *The Naked Roommate: And 107 Other Issues You Might Run into in College*. Naperville, IL: Sourcebooks.

Cole, D., & Ahmadi, S. (2010). Reconsidering campus diversity: An examination of Muslim students experiences. *The Journal of Higher Education, 81*(2): 121–139.

Crowell, D.H., & Dole, A.A. (1957). Animism and college students. *The Journal of Educational Research, 50*(5):391–395.

Diamond, L. (2001). *The Peace Book: 108 Simple Ways to Create a More Peaceful World*. Bristol, VT: The Peace Company.

Diouf, S. (1998). *Servants of Allah: African Muslims Enslaved in the Americas*. New York, NY: New York University Press.

Drywater-Whitekiller, V. (2010). Cultural resilience: Voices of Native American students in college retention. *The Canadian Journal of Native Studies, 30*(1), 1–19.

Ferguson, K.M., & Thomas-Rashid, T.L. (2011). Multicultural services at private, liberal arts colleges. In D.L. Stewart (ed.) *Multicultural Student Services on Campus: Building Bridges, Re-visioning Community*. Sterling, Virginia: Stylus Publishing LLC.

Ferrante, J. (2008). *Sociology: A Global Perspective*. Belmont, CA: Thomson Higher Education.

Flood, G. (2015). *The Bhagavad Gita*. New York, NY: W.W. Norton and Company.

GhaneaBassiri, K. (2010). *A History of Islam in America*. New York, NY: Cambridge University Press.

Giles, D. (2011). A case of forbidding academic engagement of Muslim and Jewish beliefs about the Holy Land. *Arab Studies Quarterly, 33*(3/4), 217–227.

Greenberg, M. (1961). Social characteristics of the Jewish students at the University of Maryland. *Jewish Social Studies, 23*(1), 21–37.

Katz, J.H. (1989). The challenge of diversity. In C. Woolbright (ed.) *Valuing Diversity on Campus: A Multicultural Approach.* Bloomington, IN: Association of College Unions International.

Knapp, P. (1994). *One World, Many Worlds: Contemporary Sociological Theory.* New York, NY: Harper Collins College Publishers.

Mansau, P. (2015, February 9). The Muslims of Early America. *New York Times.* Retrieved from www.nytimes.com/2015/02/09/opinion/the-founding-muslims. html?_r=0.

Maruoka, E. (2008). Wearing "Our Sword": Post-September 11 activism among South Asian Muslim women student organizations in New York. *Social Justice, 35*(2), 119–133.

McCoy, D.L. (2011). Multicultural student services at public institutions. In D.L. Stewart (ed.) *Multicultural Student Services on Campus: Building Bridges, Re-visioning Community.* Sterling, Virginia: Stylus Publishing LLC.

McKin, R. (2012). *On Religious Diversity.* New York, NY: Oxford University Press.

Mir, S. (2014). *Muslim American Women on Campus: Undergraduate Social Life and Identity.* Chapel Hill, NC: The University of North Carolina Press.

Mogahed, Y. (2012). *Reclaim Your Heart: Personal Insights on Breaking Free from Life's Shackles.* San Clemente, CA: FB Publishing.

Naropa University. (2015). Retrieved from www.naropa.edu.

Nasir, N.I.S., & Al-Amin, J. (2006). Creating identity-safe spaces on college campuses for Muslim students. *Change: The Magazine of Higher Learning, 38*(2), 22–27.

Patten, T.A., & Rice, N.D. (2009). Religious minorities and persistence at a systematic religiously-affiliated university. *Christian Higher Education, 8,* 42–53.

Riding In, L.D., & Longwell-Grice R. (2011). Multicultural student services at minority-serving institutions: Tribal colleges. In D.L. Stewart (ed.) *Multicultural Student Services on Campus: Building Bridges, Re-visioning Community.* Sterling, Virginia: Stylus Publishing LLC.

Rome, K. (2011). Multicultural student services at minority-serving institutions: Historically Black institutions. In D.L. Stewart (ed.) *Multicultural Student Services on Campus: Building Bridges, Re-visioning Community.* Sterling, Virginia: Stylus Publishing LLC.

Schmalzbauer, J. (2013). Campus religious life in America: Revitalization and renewal. *Society, 50,* 115–131.

Schoem, D. (2010). College knowledge for the Jewish Student: 101 tips. Retrieved from www.press.umich.edu/2284365/college_knowledge_for_the_jewish_studentAnn Arbor.

Segal, B.E. (1965). Contact, compliance, and distance among Jewish and non-Jewish undergraduates. *Social Problems, 13*(1), 66–74.

Stedman, C.D. (2011). Youth voices: Why interfaith work must happen on college campuses. *Journal of College and Character, 12*(1).

Storch, T. (2015). *Buddhist-Based Universities in the United States: Searching for a New Model of Higher Education.* Lanham, MD: Lexington Books.

Swatos, W.H. (1998). *Encyclopedia of Religion and Society.* Lanham, MD: Rowman & Littlefield.

The University of North Carolina Chapel Hill News. (2015). Retrieved from http://uncnews.unc.edu/2015/02/11/events-scheduled-tonight-feb-11-remember-slain-students/.

Twenge, J.M., & Campbell, W.K. (2009). *The Narcissism Epidemic: Living in the Age of Entitlement.* New York, NY: Simon & Schuster.

Wattles, J. (1996). *The Golden Rule.* New York, NY: Oxford University Press.

West, C. (2005). *Democracy Matters: Winning the Fight Against Imperialism.* New York, NY: Penguin Group.

Williams, R.H., & Vashi, G. (2007). "Hijab" and American Muslim women: Creating the space or autonomous selves. *Sociology of Religion, 68*(3), 269–287.

Winkle-Wagner, R., & Locks, A. (2013). *Diversity and Inclusion on Campus: Supporting Racially and Ethnically Underrepresented Students.* New York, NY: Routledge.

Yusuf, H. (2012). *Purification of the Heart: Signs, Symptoms and Cures of the Spiritual Diseases of the Heart.* San Francisco, CA: Sandala.

Zamani-Gallaher, E.M., & Bazile, S. (2011). Multicultural student services at community colleges. In D.L. Stewart (ed.) *Multicultural Student Services on Campus: Building Bridges, Re-visioning Community.* Sterling, Virginia: Stylus Publishing LLC.

FURTHER READING

Abdel-Khalek, A.M. (2010). Quality of life, subjective well-being, and religiosity in Muslim college students. *Quality of Life Research, 19*(8), 1133–1143.

Ancis, J.R., Sedlacek, W.E., & Mohr, J.J. (2000). Student perceptions of campus cultural climate by race. *Journal of Counseling and Development, 78,* 180–185.

Atiyat, Z.N. (2006). Student teaching at ground zero: One Muslim woman's challenge. *The English Journal, 96*(2), 14–15.

Green, M.F. (1989). *Minorities on Campus: A Handbook for Enhancing Diversity.* American Council on Education, Washington, DC: American Council on Education.

Habitegiyorgis, T.T. (2010). *Ethnic Diversity and Campus Students from Multicultural Perspectives: Learning and Cross-Cultural Experiences.* Saarbrücken, Germany: VDM Verlag Dr. Muller.

Hernandez, Y. (2013). *Latino Students' Perceptions of the University Campus Climate: Exploratory Study of First Generation Students.* Claremont, CA: Claremont Graduate University.

Jandali, A.K. (2013). Muslim students in post 9/11 classrooms: Interventions that can stem stereotypes and bullying that accompany Islamophobia in schools. *School Administrator, 69,* 32–35.

Norton, S.W., & Tomal, A. (2009). Religion and female educational attainment. *Journal of Money, Credit and Banking, 41*(5), 961–986.

Parker, M., & Sager, J. (2007). *Becoming Multiculturally Responsible on Campus: From Awareness to Action.* Independence, KY: Cengage Learning.

Patel, C.J., & Shikongo, A.E.E. (2006). Handling spirituality/religion in professional training: Experiences of a sample of Muslim college students. *Journal of Religion and Health, 45*(1), 93–112.

Pope, R.L., Reynolds, A.L., Mueller, J.A., & Musil, M. (2014). *Creating Multicultural Change on Campus.* San Francisco, CA: Jossey-Bass.

Sidanius, J., Levin, S., Van Larr, C., & Sears, D.O. (2008). The Diversity Challenge: Social Identity and Intergroup Relations on the College Campus. New York, NY: Russell Sage Foundation.

Woolbright, C. (1989). *Valuing Diversity on Campus: A Multicultural Approach.* Bloomington, IN: Association of College Unions-International.

Assessment and Strategic Planning for Campus Religious Diversity

Before student affairs practitioners can work to meet the needs of religious minorities, adequate assessment of the campus religious and spiritual environment must occur. Chapter 3 will emphasize the impact of campus climate on the religious minority student experience, discuss campus climate assessment in regards to religious minorities and interfaith programming, and discuss the implementation of assessment findings into strategic plans. In particular, this chapter will discuss the appropriateness of various assessment methods for different campus types as well as outline the diversity strategic planning process. For example, a public institution in an urban area with a large commuter population will have different assessment needs as well as different religious diversity goals than a religiously affiliated college in a rural area with a primarily residential population. The religious diversity assessment needs of each institution can be determined by its institutional type (public or private), religious affiliation (if any), and location (urban, rural, suburban). Public institutions may be more hesitant to address religious diversity in an effort to maintain the separation of church and state in public higher education. Most private institutions have religious roots even if they are currently not affiliated with any religion or denomination. Religiously affiliated institutions may be concerned with maintaining their religious identity while meeting the needs of a religiously diverse campus community. Rural institutions may not be in the vicinity of a diverse selection of houses of worship as urban institutions might be. The aforementioned issues impact the religious diversity assessment needs of higher education institutions.

DEFINING CAMPUS CLIMATE

There are several definitions for campus climate in higher education literature. A basic definition for climate is the prevailing condition of a campus.

According to Reason (2013), campus climate is exemplified by the following characteristics:

- It is multi-faceted.
- It includes attitudes and behaviors.
- It is more flexible than culture.
- It is dictated by institutional policies and practices.

Campus culture and campus climate could be used interchangeably. The reader may even assume the two terms are congruent. However, culture and climate are not the same. Climate is characterized by attitudes and standards while culture is exemplified in beliefs and habits. Phrased another way, climate is exemplified in words while culture is exemplified in actions. Peterson and Spencer (1990, p. 7) define climate as the common patterns of important dimensions of organizational life or its members' perceptions of and attitudes toward those dimensions. Institutional policies may be in place but the culture of particular departments and divisions may prevent those policies from being enacted. For example, a campus may take a secular stance on prayer while the football coach prefers to start each game with the Lord's Prayer. Issues related to sports and religious participation are too lengthy to include here and will be further addressed in Chapter 5.

Assessments can uncover many issues on campus that may otherwise go unnoticed. Divisions on campus can also be assessed, such as fraternity and sorority life, residence life, and athletics. Football is customarily referred to as religion in the South. Specifically under athletics, questions may be raised such as: Should football coaches just focus on athletics? Should how a coach motivates his or her students matter? Should sport and religion intertwine with each other at public universities? Furthermore, it is unclear what the experiences of religious minority students are who are members of sports teams, fraternities and sororities, and who participate in residence life.

Perhaps a weather analogy is most appropriate for describing campus climate. An institution with a climate that supports religious diversity can withstand a hurricane of discriminatory incidents and micro aggressions and can handle these types of occurrences with positive outcomes. In contrast, institutions with a climate that does not support religious diversity will suffer more damage from a proverbial hurricane of discriminatory incidents and micro aggressions.

Petersen and Spencer (1990) suggest that campus climate is multi-faceted and can be identified by three main dimensions of institutional climate: objective, perceived, and psychological (see Figure 3.1). These dimensions do not manifest independently. Rather, observable behaviors tend to create internal, consistent images regarding religion. These images then impact

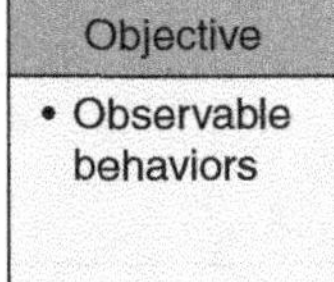

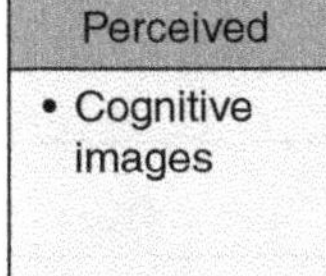

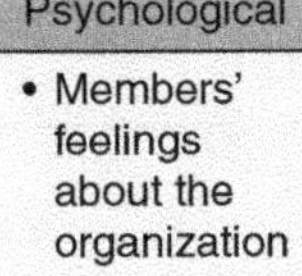

Figure 3.1 Petersen and Spencer's (1990) Three Dimensions of Institutional Climate

students and other stakeholders' feelings about the institution. Observable behaviors such as micro aggressions can also directly impact students' feelings about their institution.

Observable behaviors are actions or patterns of actions that impact religious minorities. They can be categorized into actions of faculty and staff, students, and institutional practices. Micro aggressions are also observable behaviors. Some examples of observable behaviors that stand in stark contrast to micro aggressions are providing meals after cafeteria hours for Muslim students during Ramadan, scheduling homecoming week away from Yom Kippur, and inviting a representative of a religious minority faith to offer a prayer or affirmation at a campus event. Collectively, these behaviors may create an image of religious inclusivity for a college or university.

Hurtado, Carter, and Kardia's (1998) racial climate framework, seen in Figure 3.2, is adaptable to religious diversity. This framework has four components: traditions of bias and exclusion, structural diversity (representation of religious minority students, faculty, and staff), psychological climate (perceptions of discrimination and micro aggressions), and a behavioral dimension (engagement with religious diversity).

A positive campus religious climate is characterized by the inclusion of religious minorities in the campus community (students, faculty, staff, etc.); curriculum and programming that acknowledges the experiences and challenges experienced by religious minorities; and a commitment to religious diversity in the institution's mission.

When students complain about micro aggressions, discrimination, and intolerance, an image of religious intolerance is created. When students of all faiths and belief systems share how they can celebrate their beliefs while engaging in campus life, an image of religious tolerance is generated. Also, institutions may create their own image of religious tolerance or intolerance based on informational brochures and information supplied to the media. For example, recruitment brochures reflecting actual students in religious attire and press releases about the observance of religious minority holidays on campus may serve to promote a more religiously tolerant campus atmosphere. The term "actual" to describe students in recruitment brochures is

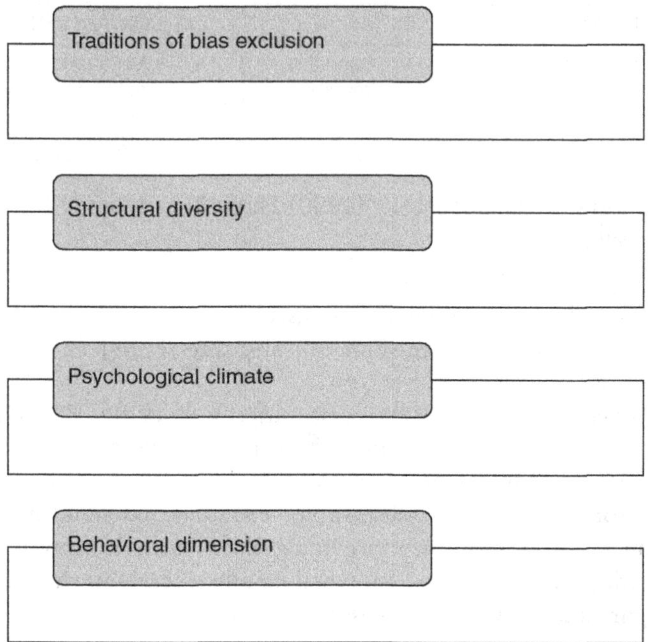

Figure 3.2 Four Components of Hurtado et al.'s (1998) Racial Climate Framework

important here, since institutions have been caught Photo-shopping brochures in an effort to make an institution appear more diverse than it actually was.

Higher education is a business and diversity is just one of the perks campuses try to sell. Institutions spend significant time and resources creating admissions guides that will attract prospective students. Diversity is just one characteristic schools wish to advertise through admissions guides. Schools can add pictures of students wearing religious attire in order to portray a religiously diverse campus. The discussion of brochures here is not to imply that pictures of students in religious attire mean a campus is religiously tolerant. However, images are important recruitment tools and valid documentation of campus climate. Actions and pictures can conflict. Also, students' feelings about their institution can conflict with the images projected. Cognitive images include images that consciously or unconsciously persist about an institution.

The University of Wisconsin is one university exposed for cutting and pasting pictures of minority students into admissions paraphernalia in order to make the campus appear more diverse (Prichep, 2013). The decision to paste a random student's face to a photo of Wisconsin students may have been one member of staff's inappropriate choice and not an entire reflection of admissions marketing at Wisconsin. However, the culture of the institution encouraged an image of diversity, even if it was a false image that allowed the member of staff responsible to think it was acceptable to cut and paste a photo of a Black student on the front of an admissions guide. However, carefully constructed images of diversity may not be completely negative. Photo-shopped diversity could demonstrate that a campus is striving to become more diverse and wishes to attract a more diverse student body rather than portray a diverse student body. Campus images should reasonably depict the diversity present on a particular campus. Ultimately, college campuses must create diversity that goes beyond a photograph.

A psychological component to diversity might include how religious minority students perceive their institutional climate. An anonymous survey may be a particularly useful tool to capture the perceptions and attitudes of students at a given college or university. Social media is another tool since students may post about micro aggressions, or negative incidents in class, or post complaints on the internet. The question arises whether religious minority students view campus as just a place to attend classes or do they view their respective campuses as a place where they can have a vibrant religious and spiritual life as well?

The campus climate at Duke appears to be supportive of religious diversity and interfaith cooperation. The university boasts a variety of groups for religious minorities, including but not limited to a Center for Islamic Studies, a Center for Jewish Life, and a Hindu Student Association. Duke weathered a hurricane of criticism for allowing the Muslim call to prayer, the *adhan*, to be performed from the Duke chapel bell tower. Critics insisted that, since Duke was founded on Christian principles, it should not allow the Muslim call to prayer to be performed from the Duke chapel bell tower. Those same critics were likely unaware of the campus climate that encourages a relatively vibrant campus life for religious minorities at Duke, the number of religious minorities enrolled at Duke, or the fact that the *adhan* request was initiated by Duke and not the Duke Muslim Students Association.

IMPORTANCE OF A CAMPUS CLIMATE OF RELIGIOUS DIVERSITY

Research on religious minority college students is discussed in Chapter 2. This section presents research on the experiences on religious minorities to demonstrate why assessments of campus religious diversity climates are urgently needed. Sorrentino (2010) gives a broad objective for assessing campus religious climate: "The raison d'être of an academic institution is education. We must decide how religion and religious diversity fits into that goal" (p. 79). Assessment of the campus religious diversity climate can also answer the following questions: How do we enhance learning by exposing students to various forms of religion? How do we respect differences among the religious, the less clearly defined "spiritual" and the irreligious? How do we help members of various religions and beliefs engage around what they have in common?

As campuses become more religiously diverse, the need to assess the campus religious climate increases. According to Bowman and Small (2010), spiritual development may be one of the most important outcomes of the college experience. Also, religious minority students are confronted with a lack of understanding of their religion by faculty, staff, and other students. Students of all religious backgrounds and belief traditions need the opportunity to develop their spirituality.

> Increases in diverse groups of students have led to both conflict and new campus opportunities for students to learn how to live and work in a complex society. Assessing the climate for diversity becomes key for institutions that wish to create comfortable, diverse learning environments.
>
> (Hurtado et al., 1998, p. 53)

Moreover, assessment needs definitely vary according to institutional type. Secular institutions will have assessment needs different from Christian or religiously affiliated institutions. Bowman and Small explain:

> At secular institutions, double minority students exhibit spiritual development similar to that of mainline Christian students. Because double minority students, by definition, are part of a minority religious group in American society, many of these students are probably accustomed to this marginalized status regardless of whether it occurs within or outside of a secular school. As a result, at secular institutions, their spiritual development is similar to that of mainline Christians. In contrast, being a double minority student at a religiously affiliated institution is negatively related to spiritual development, particularly at Catholic institutions.
>
> (2010, p. 608)

Religious minority status is associated with lower persistence levels. At religiously affiliated institutions, religious minority students are less likely to persist through college. Patten and Rice (2009) found a significant difference in persistence from the freshman to sophomore year between college students who identify with the religion affiliated with the school and students who did not. Religious minority staff and faculty may experience discomfort at religiously affiliated colleges. Shriberg and Wester (1994) found that non-Catholic student affairs professionals at a Catholic institution reported that they felt uncomfortable in many situations and that their religious beliefs negatively affected their careers. Though students are not specifically addressed, the aforementioned research demonstrates that religiously affiliated institutions may be particularly challenged in accommodating students and faculty who may be religious minorities on that particular campus (e.g., non-Catholics at a Catholic institution). Student affairs staff at a Catholic institution may feel constrained in their efforts to serve non-Catholic students.

Campus climate can support or impede student outcomes. Pascarella and Terenzini (2005) link discriminatory campus climates to a decreased likelihood of persistence among students.

Assessment of campus climate in relation to religion and spirituality is important because religious minorities have decreased spiritual well-being when compared to religious majority students (Bowman & Small, 2013). Spiritual well-being is important for student development and persistence. According to Kuh and Gonyea (2006), students who engage in spirituality enhancing practices are more engaged on campus. Engagement is a huge buzz word in higher education. We should want all students to be engaging in spirituality practices, regardless of their faith. The aforementioned research does not address religious minorities such as Atheists.

Atheists do not believe in a god or gods or any supernatural existence. According to Converse (2003), there are three types of Atheists. The first type simply accepts that god does not exist. The second type accepts that god does not exist and reasons how god does not exist. The third type of Atheist acknowledges that god does not exist, explains how god does not exist, publicly claims that god does not exist and structures their lifestyle around Atheism. Atheists may also be identified by these terms: secular humanist, nonbeliever, naturalist, or free thinker (Goodman & Mueller, 2009). Atheists also determine what is morally right and wrong by what is good for humankind, without support from scripture.

In a study of undergraduates at 28 institutions, Bowman and Smedley (2012) discovered that Protestant students had the highest levels of satisfaction while students from marginalized religions or no religion at all had the lowest levels of satisfaction. Issues of dissatisfaction are not limited to religious minorities. Strongly committed religious majority students, such as evangelical Christians, may also experience a hostile campus environment (Mayhew, Bowman, & Rockenbach, 2014). According to the aforementioned study, it appears that the highest levels of dissatisfaction occur at opposite ends of the religious spectrum: the deeply religious and those who are not religious at all. A religious diversity campus climate assessment would address the issues of conservative Christians and others of the religious majority who may experience hostility because of their ideas and values.

Small and Bowman (2013) determined that religious majority students experienced increased religious commitment and decreased religious skepticism compared to religious minority students. This section highlights the religious diversity issues that calls for a religious diversity campus climate study.

U.S. Supreme Court Justice Lewis Powell addressed diversity in his defining opinion of the 1978 *Regents of the University of California* v. *Bakke*: "It is not too much to say that the nation's future depends upon leaders trained through wide exposure to the ideas and mores of students as diverse as this Nation of many peoples." Though the *Bakke* case dealt with racial diversity, Justice Powell's use of the words "ideas" and "mores" is undeniably relevant to religious diversity. Ideas and mores are what differentiates religions and worldviews from each other. The arguments for diversity, including religious diversity, are compelling.

There are a range of characteristics an assessment of religious diversity climate should assess. Out-group stress is one characteristic that an assessment of campus religious diversity climate should assess. Religious minorities may be subject to out-group stress. Abouguendia and Noels (2001) define out-group stress as tension associated with the particular nature of interactions that ethnic communities often have with members of mainstream society, such as discrimination, prejudice, and stereotyping. Effects of out-group stress can include higher incidences of depression and low self-esteem. (Abbas 2002). Religious minorities can certainly be considered an out group since they practice a different faith from the majority of their campuses and the larger society. As one can imagine, depression and low self-esteem are not conducive to student persistence or satisfaction. Campus climate assessment should address the micro level of religious diversity in the form of friendships. Though friendships and relationships are not directly related to campus climate, the macro level (campus) environment could impact the micro level, as seen in friendships between religious minority and majority students.

There are two types of religious diversity for campuses to assess and encourage: interactional diversity and classroom diversity. Gurin, Dey, Gurin, and Hurtado (2003) define these two diversity types. "Informal interactional diversity is the actual experience students have with diverse peers in the campus environment. Classroom diversity is exposure to knowledge about race and ethnicity in formal classrooms" (p. 23). Learning is minimal when students are surrounded by others who are just like themselves. The religion course is not the only classroom experience where students may be exposed to knowledge about religion. Disciplines such as English, Political Science, or Sociology are additional opportunities to address religious minority faiths.

INITIATING AN ASSESSMENT OF CAMPUS RELIGIOUS DIVERSITY CLIMATE

The following questions can guide the assessment of campus religious and spiritual life. These questions are adapted from Goodman and Mueller (2009).

- Does your campus provide opportunities for personal development beyond Christianity and beyond religion?
- Do forums for religious inquiry value knowledge and perspectives outside of mainline Protestant Christianity?
- How have faculty and administrators addressed religious diversity?

Institutions must first establish who is a religious minority in the context of their institution. For the discussions in this text, a student is considered Christian if they believe in Jesus Christ as their Lord and Savior, the teachings of the Old and New Testaments, and the Holy Trinity and the resurrection of Christ (Schlosser, 2003). At the majority of post-secondary institutions in the United States, any student who is not Christian is considered a religious minority. However, there are some smaller Christian denominations, such as Seventh Day Adventists and Latter-Day Saints Mormons, that can be considered a part of the religious minority. In any educational institution, from pre-kindergarten to college, educators must know who their students are and what they believe. One cannot teach, educate, or serve without knowing their students' background. Religion is an important part of a student's background. In some ways, student affairs practitioners are educators and instructors as much as faculty and grade school teachers. Student affairs practitioners promote equal representation of religious minority students and address issues of religious diversity through co-curricular programming, in addition to counseling students and providing opportunities for students to engage. These opportunities must be geared toward students' needs and backgrounds. Through their positions, student affairs practitioners shape the religious environment by promoting the representation of religious minorities on campus. Diversity is an overriding principle of the student affairs profession. Moreover, student affairs practitioners are the socializing agents of the campus environment. Executive-level administrators on college campuses should be concerned with assessing the interfaith competence of student affairs practitioners. The results of such assessments will help student affairs units determine the goals and objectives of an interfaith development program. They guide students. So, these opportunities must be geared toward students' needs and backgrounds. Develop well-rounded students and expose religious majority students to other faiths.

The admissions application is an ideal place to ask about prospective students' religious faith, just like students are asked to indicate their race or ethnicity. The application should clearly indicate that answering a question about religion is voluntary. Data from this application question and a question from a survey of entering students can be used to compare the religious background of applicants to the religious background of students who ultimately enroll. Those statistics could highlight large groups of students from particular religious backgrounds who apply to an institution but ultimately decide not to enroll. An institution may have a large percentage of religious minorities applying but a similar percentage is ultimately not represented in the freshman class. Results such as these could indicate that students from a particular religious minority apply to an institution but ultimately decide not to attend because they do not perceive the institution as religiously inclusive. Additional data collection could determine why sizeable groups of religious minority students are dissuaded from attending a particular institution.

Learning the religious or spiritual background of students is a primary use for a religious survey. A sample question could read like this:

What religious, spiritual, or belief tradition do you subscribe to, if any?

A. Buddhism
B. Christianity (if selected, please indicate Protestant or Catholic)

    a. Protestant

        i.   Denomination, if any_______________________________________

    b. Catholic

C. Hinduism
D. Islam
E. Judaism
F. Other (Please list)_______________________________________
G. Spiritual, but not religious
H. Atheism
I. Agnosticism
J. None
K. Prefer not to respond

Who is a minority and what is diversity can be different for every college or university. Though Whites are not a racial minority in the United States, they are certainly racial minorities at HBCUs (Historically Black Colleges or Universities) or predominately Black institutions. One religious group could be a minority on campus but a section of the religious majority off campus. Evangelical Christians, for example, are one such group. Bowman and Small

(2013) define double religious minorities as students who are religious minorities on and off campus. Double religious minorities generally include students who identify as Buddhist, Eastern Orthodox, Hindu, Muslim, Jewish, Latter-day Saints (LDS) Mormon, Quaker, Seventh Day Adventist, Unitarian/Universalist, and other non-Christian faith believers as well as non-believers.

Since campus climate is more flexible than campus culture, a climate that is supportive of religious minorities can override aspects of religious bias and privilege that may proliferate in the campus culture. Culture is impacted by a campus's history and traditions and that history and those traditions may have been bolstered by Christian norms. For example, Duke University is a private, religiously unaffiliated institution. However, it was founded and supported by the Methodist church and maintains the historic Duke Chapel. Though Duke is not officially affiliated with any religion or denomination, the chapel remains an iconic centerpiece of the campus. On college campuses that do maintain a chapel on campus, it is an important building, whether the institution is religiously affiliated or not. The Memorial Chapel, listed on the National Register of Historic Landmarks, on the campus of Hampton University is another prolific campus chapel. Hampton is also religiously unaffiliated. Religiously unaffiliated institutions should acknowledge the Christian or denominational influence on their campuses. To say a campus is religiously unaffiliated can deny an institution's history and traditions that may be grounded in Christianity. Maybe colleges should say they are religiously unaffiliated with Christian influences. Perhaps the religious affiliation of college campuses refers to its sponsorship and control, not its traditions and climate.

Now that campus climate is defined, methods for its assessment will be discussed. Survey research reaches larger numbers of respondents while focus groups extract intimate responses from participants. "Among the greatest strengths of the focus group method is its capacity to harness the power of human interaction by capitalizing on relationships and consequently generating insights that might not otherwise emerge" (Dreachslin, 1998). A focus group can expand on findings from a quantitative survey. Specifically, survey responses can guide focus group questions. Moreover, focus group responses can help guide a strategic plan for campus religious diversity.

Qualitative research in general and focus groups in particular give a voice to participants that is not present with surveys. This makes qualitative research particularly useful for examining an issue that has diversity implications, like religion. A focus group is an optimal tool for assessing the experiences of religious minorities on campus since students tend to speak more freely in focus groups. A pilot study will help a focus group be the most effective by providing an opportunity to test questions and work out logistics.

Based on survey responses, focus group questions can focus on positive and negative aspects of religious diversity on campus, religious minority student interactions with faculty, staff and other students, and opportunities to improve religious diversity. Incentives are one way to recruit participation into surveys and focus groups. The focus group session can start with an open-ended questionnaire. Here are sample questions to begin a focus group. These questions are adapted from Goodman and Mueller (2009).

1. Write down three things you appreciate about religious diversity on this campus.
2. Write down three things that disappoint you about the climate of religious diversity on this campus.
3. What are the interactions between Christians and non-Christians like on this campus?
4. If you could change one thing about the religious climate on this campus, what would it be?

Before interfaith education and programming, institutions should provide the opportunity for students to have their religious knowledge voluntarily assessed. In order to create a campus climate that is religiously tolerant and inclusive, institutions must understand what students, as well as the entire campus community, know about religion and belief perspectives outside of mainline Christianity, non-Christian religions and other belief perspectives. Bias and intolerance of religious minorities is bred by ignorance and unfamiliarity.

Below is a survey that could be used to assess religious knowledge. This assessment can be used as a survey. Ideally, a survey is used and then followed up with a focus group. Surveys have been the main methodology for assessing campus climate (Phillips Morrow, Burris-Kitchen, & Der-Karabetian, 2000). Survey research provides breadth while focus groups provide depth. Also, the questions in this survey can be rearranged to use in a Jeopardy or quiz bowl format. The jeopardy or game night will be more appropriate for smaller campuses and intimate groups on larger campuses. Student affairs professionals can use the format of these questions to add more questions about religion. The following survey is useful for assessing knowledge of minority religions. It is adapted from the Pew Research Center Religion and Public Life U.S. Religious Knowledge Quiz (2010).

1. When does the Jewish Sabbath begin?

   a. Friday
   b. Saturday
   c. Wednesday
   d. Thursday night at sundown

2. What is Ramadan?

    a. The Hindu festival of lights
    b. A Jewish day of atonement
    c. The Islamic holy month
    d. The month of Prophet Muhammad's birthday

3. In which religion are Vishnu and Shiva central figures?

    a. Islam
    b. Hinduism
    c. Taoism
    d. Buddhism

4. What was Joseph Smith's religion?

    a. Catholic
    b. Jewish
    c. Buddhist
    d. Mormon

5. What religion do most people in Pakistan consider themselves?

    a. Buddhism
    b. Hinduism
    c. Islam
    d. Christianity

6. Which of these religions aims at nirvana, the state of being free from suffering?

    a. Islam
    b. Buddhism
    c. Hinduism
    d. Baha'i

7. What religion do most people in Indonesia consider themselves?

    a. Catholicism
    b. Hinduism
    c. Judaism
    d. Islam

8. The Jewish holy book is called:

    a. Qur'an
    b. Torah
    c. Hadith
    d. Hebrew

9. If you are from India, you are most likely:

    a. Hindu
    b. Muslim
    c. Sikh
    d. Jewish

10. _____________ believe God does not exist.

    a. Agnostics
    b. Humanists
    c. Atheists

Assessment can have multiple goals, including but not limited to: 1) assessment of the religious knowledge of the campus population (i.e., knowledge of religious minority groups), and 2) assessment of the campus environment toward religious minorities. Ideally, the entire campus (students, staff, faculty, and administrators) should be involved in campus assessment and should have the opportunity to contribute their perspectives. Faculty, staff, and administrator responses and perspectives may be useful in understanding why the needs of religious minorities go unmet. Campus climate assessments can help practitioners deal with religious minority issues with the goal of having a more inclusive campus.

Both religious minorities and religious majorities may desire and benefit from interreligious experiences and contacts. However, they may want these experiences on different terms. For example, religious minorities may want more institutional commitments and programs while the religious majority may want more personal connections developed on their own but facilitated by student affairs personnel. Furthermore, religious minority students may want to notice institutional support demonstrated, while religious majority students may not want to feel obligated to appreciate other religions. A survey of student experiences and preferences for interreligious contact can determine how students want to interact with those who believe differently from themselves.

The student population should be surveyed at different levels of their experience. Whether graduating, continuing, or enrolling for the first time, students at every level have a unique and valuable perspective to offer regarding the religious climate of their respective college or university. Institutions of higher education can be more proactive about student input by surveying seniors and recent graduates about their experiences of religious diversity, with a particular focus on the campus environment. Perhaps students view the campus as too secular, making it awkward to discuss religion for both Christians and non-Christians alike. Entering students can be surveyed for their religious knowledge and their expectations as far as campus religious and spiritual life.

The Campus Religious and Spiritual Climate Survey, created by Dr. Alyssa Rockenbach and Dr. Mathew Mayhew, is one survey institutions can employ to assess campus religious and spiritual climate. This survey helps the student affairs practitioner develop an inclusive campus climate that supports all beliefs and viewpoints. The climate scales on the survey are adapted from a framework that models interrelated aspects of campus racial/ethnic diversity.

The results of campus religious diversity assessments must be implemented into a plan to develop a more inclusive community. Hurtado et al. (1998) elaborate the following point: "Once a decision is made to conduct a climate study of diversity on campus, the most important step is developing a plan of action that will follow the climate assessment" (p. 61). This step is most important for religious minorities as they may feel further alienation if no changes follow the assessment. Institutions must also ensure that assessment results are widely disseminated. It should be noted that an adept plan must involve executive-level administrators.

RELIGIOUS DIVERSITY STRATEGIC PLANNING

Almost every institution of higher learning has developed a strategic plan at some point in its history. Strategic plans help institutions meet goals, such as increasing enrollment or increasing diversity. Once climate assessments are complete, institutions can develop strategic plans based on the results of the assessment. Assessment results will tell an institution where it needs to go in regards to religious diversity. The strategic plan will then tell the institution how to get where it needs to go. Many institutions already have diversity strategic plans where religious diversity is addressed. Other institutions may need to create a religious diversity strategic plan or update their current diversity strategic plan to include religion and similar worldviews. A diversity strategic plan can be adapted to specifically address improvements to a campus' religious climate.

Adapted from the Association for the Study of Higher Education's (2007) definition of a diversity strategic plan, a religious diversity strategic plan synthesizes data from a religious diversity campus climate assessment, incorporates the analysis of gaps between the current climate and the desired religious diversity climate, and situates the goals for religious diversity in the context of the institution's strategic agenda. Also, a religious diversity strategic plan communicates the importance of diversity to external and internal constituencies and ensures resources are allocated to religious diversity.

A religious diversity strategic plan should include:

- a vision statement
- input from various campus constituencies
- accountability mechanisms
- ongoing assessment
- resource allocation.

Faculty can be involved in creating a religious diversity strategic plan or including religion in a diversity strategic plan that is already created. A strategic plan will not be successful without faculty input. Faculty and student affairs staff must collaborate to implement a religious diversity strategic plan. These constituencies bring different, but valuable, perspectives and expertise. When faculty and student affairs staff work together, the religious diversity plan is more likely to be widely promoted. Cultivators of a religious diversity strategic plan should look for ways to incorporate the academic triad of teaching, research, and service in faculty contributions to the plan (Whitney, 2010). Faculty members may specifically be looking for opportunities to publish articles and secure grants related to religious diversity. Faculty who conduct research on religion, interfaith initiatives, and group differences may be particularly resourceful.

The benefits of a strategic plan are that it sets measurable goals. Additional assessment is needed after the strategic plan to see if goals were met. Also, assessment of student outcomes as a result of the implementation of a religious diversity plan should occur to ensure accountability. If institutions fail to act on climate assessment results, the opportunity for religious minorities to feel included in campus life and to have a satisfying undergraduate experience is significantly diminished. The process of religious diversity assessment and strategic planning answers the questions "Where are we now?" and "Where are we going?"

Before the religious diversity strategic planning phase begins, administrators must establish a strong need for a religious diversity plan. The need may already appear obvious to senior-level administrators. However, a shared understanding of the need for the plan is critical. More importantly, the consequences of failing to address religious diversity should be widely understood. Without it, the strategic planning process may become ineffective and tedious. One might assume that the need for a religious diversity strategic plan is established by the previously discussed campus assessments. The actual steps and expected outcomes of the strategic plan are shaped by the assessments. The need may be established by anecdotal knowledge and as a reaction to religiously motivated incidents.

The institutional mission in regards to religious diversity is discussed in Chapter 5. The mission and vision must be clear before planning can successfully commence. Tromp and Ruben (2010) refer to the five-minute elevator ride as a short speech on your institution's mission and values on religious diversity. If a prospective student who happens to be a religious minority is touring your campus and asks about how your institution meets the needs of religious minorities, how could your religious diversity mission and vision be reflected in a five-minute response? The mission of an institution, simply put, is what an institution does. The institutional vision is what your institution wants to be in the future. Questions may be raised such as: What does your institution do? Who does it educate and how? How does who it educates and how they are educated impact how you handle religious diversity? How does your vision for religious diversity fit with the vision of your institution as a whole? What objectives must be achieved in order for your institution to fulfill its vision? Once you understand what your institution does, where it is, and where it wants to go, you have distinguished the origins of your strategic plan.

Next, strategic planners must identify collaborators and beneficiaries. Ruben (2010) defines collaborators as groups an institution or department must coordinate with to carry out its mission, and beneficiaries as groups for which it provides its programs and services. For a department tasked with creating a religious diversity strategic plan, internal collaborators may be admissions personnel, residence life, campus facilities, a department of religious studies, and other departments and units within the institution. External collaborators may be places of worship in the community or non-profit organizations that support religious diversity and interfaith engagement. Alumni could also serve as external collaborators.

Along with the aforementioned focus groups and surveys as pre-assessments for strategic planning, a SWOT (Strengths, Weaknesses, Opportunities, Threats) analysis can inform strategic planners about threats against and opportunities for religious diversity initiatives on their respective campuses. There are a variety of issues for diversity strategic planners to consider. Planners should understand the current trends regarding religious diversity and the role of colleges and universities in these trends. Also, planners should understand beneficiaries' and collaborators' perceptions of your institution or department. Moreover, the most influential beneficiaries and collaborators should be identified and their perceptions of the institution or department assessed. Next, what sources of funding are available to execute a future strategic plan? What laws and policies regarding religion, free speech, student services, etc. must be considered during the strategic planning efforts. Planning leaders must candidly address the aforementioned questions and issues before proceeding with religious diversity strategic planning.

Planners should identify and prioritize three to five desired outcomes from the religious diversity strategic plan. Goals should be written in laymen's terms so they are widely understood. Goals should also be measurable. Most importantly, goals should address the critical needs identified by prior assessments.

Once a diversity strategic plan is completed and executed, its outcomes and impact must be assessed. Were the desired changes achieved? To what extent? Beneficiary (primarily students) satisfaction should be assessed. At this point, achievements should be celebrated and opportunities to achieve additional outcomes noted.

DIVERSITY STRATEGIC PLANS

The authors randomly selected the diversity strategic plans of nine institutions to see how religious diversity was addressed. The nine institutions are: the University of California-Berkeley, College of Charleston, Georgia State University, Messiah College, Pennsylvania State University-Lehigh Valley, Muhlenberg College, Dickenson College, the University of Texas at Austin, and UCLA (the University of California, Los Angeles). Religion is specifically mentioned at least as a point of difference or a protected status in eight of the nine institutions (College of Charleston, 2012; Dickinson College, 2015). The University of Texas at Austin does not specifically mention religion at all in its diversity strategic plan (University of Texas at Austin, 2011). Perhaps the absence of the mention of religion in the diversity strategic plan of Texas's flagship university is an indication of the state's Bible belt status. Despite a lack of religious diversity initiatives in its strategic plan (Georgia State University, 2011), Georgia State University has embraced interfaith engagement by accepting President Obama's Interfaith and Community Service Campus Challenge. The Interfaith Action Initiative at the University of California-Berkeley, in collaboration with a variety of campus faith-based organizations, sponsors interfaith programming. Berkeley's strategic plan, from 2009, is expired or outdated (University of California-Berkeley, 2009). Perhaps an updated plan will address interfaith initiatives. This initiative encourages students from different religious and non-religious backgrounds to join together while completing community service (White House, 2015). The Center for Spiritual and Ethical Development at Penn State-Lehigh Valley encourages an appreciation for religious and worldview diversity (Pennsylvania State University-Lehigh Valley, 2010). The College of Charleston's Religious Life Council boasts advisors from a variety of religious organizations. Moreover, the college strongly supports religious accommodation, as evidenced by its Statement on Religious Accommodation discussed in Chapter 5. Methodist-affiliated Dickenson College also supports religious inclusion with its religious holiday policy. Moreover, Dickenson does not allow college-wide events to be scheduled on the same day as a religious holiday. Muhlenberg

College, affiliated with the Lutheran Church, addresses religious diversity in its strategic plan more thoroughly than any of the other eight colleges discussed here. Religion is included in the history of diversity at Muhlenberg in its diversity strategic plan. This history highlights that Muhlenberg understands its history as far as religious diversity. The brief history reads as follows:

> Chapel attendance, a factor in the early years of a Muhlenberg education, had not been required for many years. Protestant and Roman Catholic services continue to be offered weekly, and religious diversity has continued to increase since the 1990s. Thus, religious composition of the Muhlenberg student body has changed dramatically in recent decades. Of students who currently report a religious affiliation, most belong to a variety of Protestant denominations, Judaism, or Roman Catholicism. The once large Lutheran population of European descent has dropped rapidly. By 2013, only 5.2 percent of students identified themselves as Lutheran, a smaller percentage than those who said that they had no religious affiliation. (Almost 9 percent identified as members of other Protestant denominations.) Roman Catholic students accounted for about 30 percent of students, almost 32 percent were Jewish. A small but growing number of Hindus, Buddhists, Muslims, and students of other religious traditions are part of the student body. In its Multicultural Center, Muhlenberg created one of the very few Muslim prayer rooms in an American liberal arts college, with an adjacent purpose-built bathroom for washing before praying. An Institute for Christian–Jewish Understanding was established in 1989, using academic resources to foster such research and dialogue and to build bridges of understanding. The Interfaith Leadership Council, convened by the College Chaplain is comprised of representatives from student religious organizations and other religious/spiritual affiliations. The Council offers programming for students to help build bridges between religious traditions.
>
> (Muhlenberg College, 2014a)

Muhlenberg is able to balance its Lutheran identity with its commitment to religious diversity as evidenced by the last sentence of its mission statement: "Honoring its historical heritage from the Lutheran Church and its continuing connection with the Evangelical Lutheran Church in America, Muhlenberg encourages, welcomes, and celebrates a variety of faith traditions and spiritual perspectives" (Muhlenberg College, 2014b). UCLA also discloses a breakdown of its student body by religious affiliation in its diversity strategic plan. Also, religion courses satisfy the diversity course degree requirement in the school of arts and architecture. Institutions are taking steps to maintain and increase religious inclusion in ways their diversity strategic plans do not directly indicate.

Religion is not discussed as frequently as race or sexual orientation/identity in these strategic plans. The importance of race and LGBTQ issues are very important and should not be diminished by an increased focus on religious diversity. Schools whose plans do not specifically address religious diversity is not necessarily a bad thing. They may already have interfaith programming in place. The diversity strategic plan at Messiah College, an evangelical Christian-affiliated college, identifies religious tradition as a point of diversity. However, the plan includes a clause mentioning that points of diversity are understood within the context of Messiah's mission and identity.

> Ultimately, our mission and identity help us to realize that diversity is not an end in and of itself. Rather, it is a means to intellectual, social, and spiritual renewal for individuals, communities, and society. Diversity is a crucial aspect of our educational commitment to holistic development and personal transformation. Diversity is also necessary to shaping a powerful learning environment that enlarges student capacity for critical thinking and cognitive complexity. Simultaneously, diversity is part of our response to the gospel; it is a means to becoming a reconciled community. Diversity is part of what it means to celebrate the goodness of God's creation and to renew our understanding of the reality that all of humanity reflects the signature of God. Engaging diversity is an avenue to realizing God's vision for the body of Christ in our world. The Christian community is called to practice the ministry of reconciliation by breaking down walls that separate and healing the brokenness of creation; the hope of this ministry is that the Christian community will come together as a new creation and, in doing so, offer a radical model for the world. As we consider the foundations of our diversity work and commit ourselves to what is required to fulfill our calling as a distinct Christian academic community, may we remain ever mindful of these ultimate aims and our hope for future.
>
> (Messiah College, 2013)

In this way, Messiah, as a private college, differs from the strategic diversity plans of public institutions. What we see from these plans is that, while religion is recognized as a point of diversity, there is little strategic planning toward enhancing religious diversity on these campuses. This could be for a number of reasons. Perhaps an institution has not assessed an unmet need regarding religious diversity. Perhaps an institution has assessed an unmet need regarding religious diversity, met those needs, and has not yet updated desired outcomes for a strategic plan. Or perhaps an institution has recognized anecdotally a need to address religious diversity but is, unfortunately, unconsciously waiting for a critical mass in the form of a religiously motivated incident or crime to force a response.

CONCLUSION

Connections between race and religion are made in Chapter 6. How do assessments of campus racial climates relate to religious climates? Though race and religion are connected as objects of discrimination and bias, a campus can have a racially inclusive climate that is not religiously inclusive. Multicultural affairs and centers for students of color are fairly common on today's college campuses. A campus religious climate assessment may determine if multicultural affairs offices are actually prepared to handle religious diversity.

Ultimately, colleges must view a diverse student body as a resource that must be cultivated and embraced in all forms (race, gender, religion, socioeconomic, sexual orientation, and ability). The initial investment in a religiously diverse and inclusive student body is a thorough assessment of the campus religious climate. The next step is a strategic plan based on the results of campus assessments. Ongoing assessment must occur to ensure that the goals of the strategic plan are met.

DISCUSSION QUESTIONS

1. How might the location of a university (rural/urban) affect the religious diversity of a campus?
2. What are the differences between campus culture and campus climate?
3. In your estimation, what campus characteristics would be most ideal for interreligious dialogue among faculty, staff, and students?
4. What are the potential barriers to institutional assessments of campus climate?
5. How often should campuses conduct strategic planning and assessments?
6. What are the possible consequences of the failure of university administrators to conduct assessments and strategic plans related to religious diversity?

REFERENCES

Abbas, T. (2002). The home and the school in the educational achievements of South Asians. *Race, Ethnicity and Education, 5*(3), 291–316.

Abouguendia, M., & Noels, K. (2001). General and acculturation-related daily hassles and psychological adjustment in first and second generation South Asian immigrants to Canada. *International Journal of Psychology, 36*(3), 163–173.

Association for the Study of Higher Education. (2007). Best practices in diversity planning and assessment. *ASHE Higher Education Report, 33*(1), 89–102.

Bowman, N.A., & Small, J.L. (2010). Do college students who identify with a privileged religion experience greater spiritual development? Exploring individual and institutional dynamics. *Research in Higher Education, 51*, 595–614.

Bowman, N.A., & Small, J.L. (2013). The experiences and spiritual growth of religiously privileged and religiously marginalized college students. In A. Bryant Rockenbach & M. Mayhew (eds) *Spirituality in College Students' Lives*. New York: Routledge.

Bowman, N.A., & Smedley, C.T. (2013). The forgotten minority: Examining religious affiliation and university satisfaction. *Higher Education, 65*, 745–760.

College of Charleston. (2012). *Diversity Strategic Plan*. Retrieved from http://pcdaei. cofc.edu/diversity-strategic-plan/DiversityStrategicPlan2012final.pdf.

Converse, R.W. (2003). *Atheism as a Positive Social Force*. New York, NY: Algora.

Dickenson College. (2015). *Diversity Strategic Plan for Dickenson College*. Retrieved from www.dickinson.edu/download/downloads/id/2159/diversity_strategic_plan.

Dreachslin, J.L. (1998). Conducting effective focus groups in the context of diversity: Theoretical underpinnings and practical implications. *Qualitative Health Research, 8*(6), 813–820.

Georgia State University. (2011). *Diversity Strategic Plan, 2011–2016*. Retrieved from http://odaa.gsu.edu/diversity/2011-2016-diversity-strategic-plan/.

Goodman, K.M., & Mueller, J. A. (2009). Invisible, marginalized, and stigmatized: Understanding the needs of Atheist students. *New Directions for Student Services, 125*, 55–63.

Gurin, P.Y., Dey, E.L., Gurin, G., & Hurtado, S. (2003). How does racial/ethnic diversity promote education? *The Western Journal of Black Studies, 27*(1), 20–29.

Hurtado, S., Carter, D.F., & Kardia, D. (1998). The climate for diversity: Key issues for institutional self-study. *New Directions for Institutional Research, 98*: 53–63.

Kuh, G.D., & Gonyea, R.M. (2006). Spirituality, liberal learning and college student engagement. *Liberal Education, 92*(1), 40–47.

Mayhew, M.J., Bowman, N.A., & Rockenbach, A.B. (2014). Silencing whom? Linking campus climates for religious, spiritual, and worldview diversity to student worldviews. *The Journal of Higher Education, 85*(2), 219–245.

Messiah College. (2013). *Diversity Plan: Messiah College Foundations*. Retrieved from www.messiah.edu/documents/diversity_affairs/DiversityStrategicPlan.pdf.

Muhlenberg College. (2014a). *Muhlenberg College Five Year Diversity Strategic Plan*. Retrieved from www.muhlenberg.edu/media/contentassets/pdf/president/initiatives/Diversity%20Strategic%20Plan%20-%20Final%20Approved%20Version.pdf.

Muhlenberg College. (2014b). *Muhlenberg College Mission Statement*. Retrieved from www.muhlenberg.edu/main/aboutus/mission.html.

Pascarella, E., & Terenzini, P. (2005). *How College Affects Students: A Third Decade of Research*. Indianapolis, IN: Jossey-Bass.

Patten, T.A., & Rice, D.N. (2009). Religious minorities and persistence at a systemic religiously-affiliated university. *Christian Higher Education, 8*, 42–53.

Pennsylvania State University-Lehigh Valley. (2010). *Penn State Lehigh Valley Diversity Strategic Plan*. Retrieved from https://institutionalplanninglv.files.wordpress.com/2011/05/psulv_dsp_2010-2015.pdf.

Petersen, M.W., & Spencer, M.G. (1990). Understanding academic culture and climate. In W.G. Tierney (ed.) *Assessing Academic Climates and Cultures*. San Francisco, CA: Jossey-Bass.

Pew Research Center. (2010). *U.S. Religious Knowledge Survey*. Retrieved from www.pewforum.org/2010/09/28/u-s-religious-knowledge-survey/.

Phillips Morrow, G., Burris-Kitchen, D., & Der-Karabetian, A. (2000). Assessing campus climate of cultural diversity: A focus on focus groups. *College Student Journal, 34*(4), 589–604.

Pricep, D. (2013, December 29). A campus more colorful than reality: Beware that college brochure. *National Public Radio*. Retrieved from www.npr.org/2013/12/29/257765543/a-campus-more-colorful-than-reality-beware-that-college-brochure?utm_source=npr_newsletter&utm_medium=email&utm_content=20150528&ut m_campaign=npr_email_a_friend&utm_term=storyshare.

Reason, R. (2013). Creating and assessing campus climates that support personal and social responsibility. *Liberal Education, 99*(1), 38–43.

Regents of the University of California v. *Bakke*, 438 U.S. 265 (1978).

Ruben, B.D. (2010). *Excellence in Higher Education Guide: An Integrated Approach to Assessment, Planning and Improvement in Colleges and Universities*. Washington, DC: National Association of College and University Business Advisors.

Schlosser, L.Z. (2003). Christian privilege: Breaking a sacred taboo. *Journal of Multicultural Counseling and Development, 31*, 44–51.

Shriberg, A., & Wester, S. (1994). Employment satisfaction among non-Catholic student affairs professionals at Catholic colleges and universities. *Journal of College Student Development, 35*(2), 109–120.

Small, J.L., & Bowman, N.A. (2013). Religious commitment, skepticism, and struggle among U.S. college students: The impact of majority/minority religious affiliation and institutional type. *Journal for the Scientific Study of Religion, 50*(1): 154–174.

Sorrentino, P.V. (2010). What do college students want? A student centered approach to multifaith involvement. *Journal of Ecumenical Studies, 45*(1), 79–96.

Tromp, S.A., & Ruben, B.D. (2010). *Strategic Planning in Higher Education: A Guide for Leaders.* Washington: DC, National Association of College and University Business Officers.

University of California-Berkeley. (2009). *UC Berkeley Strategic Plan for Equity, Inclusion, and Diversity: Pathway to Excellence.* Retrieved from http://diversity.berkeley.edu/sites/default/files/SPEID_FINAL_webversion.pdf

University of Texas at Austin. (2011) *Strategic Plan 2011–2016.* Retrieved from http://ddce.utexas.edu/2016/wp-content/uploads/2012/02/DDCE_StrategicPlan_020212.pdf.

White House. (2015). *The President's Interfaith and Community Service Campus Challenge.* Retrieved from www.whitehouse.gov/administration/eop/ofbnp/interfaith-service.

Whitney, R. (2010). Involving academic faculty in developing and implementing a strategic plan. *New Directions for Student Services, 132*, 63–74.

Minority Faith in the Classroom

There is a demonstrated need for the study of world religions. The average score on a religious knowledge survey administered by the Pew Forum on Religion and Public Life (2010) is 50% – a failing grade. Even though student affairs personnel primarily deal with student experiences outside of the classroom, the classroom can play an integral role in student satisfaction. Chapter 4 will discuss how religion is taught in reference to minority religions. Student affairs practitioners and faculty can work together to ensure classrooms are welcoming spaces for religious minorities. Discontent with the classroom can carry over outside the classroom into the domain of the student affairs practitioner. Also, the campus culture in regards to religious diversity will permeate into the classroom.

First-year orientation is like a classroom experience because students are expected to learn or gain ideas. As orientations touch on diversity, diversity awareness should not be limited to race. Religious diversity should be added to orientation programming, where it does not already exist. Orientation should expose Christians to minority religions and worldviews and demonstrate religious inclusion to religious minorities and introduce opportunities for interfaith engagement for everyone. The freshman seminar is an optimal opportunity to introduce and encourage the exploration of religious pluralism and interfaith engagement by assigning readings from diverse religious perspectives. Mention of first-year students here includes first-year community college students. Community colleges enroll about half of all college students in the United States. First-year community college students are in no less need of knowledge about world religions than baccalaureate students.

Though this book primarily deals with religious diversity in a student affairs setting, the authors thought it was important to include a chapter on the challenges for religious diversity and religious minorities in the classroom. The classroom can play an integral part in welcoming, supporting, and validating religious minority students. Faculty have a role in fostering the spiritual development of students. According to Bowman and Small (2013), students' spiritual development is encouraged when faculty support students in their religious beliefs and engage students in conversation about their religious beliefs.

Elshtain (2002) argues that teaching always reflects the religious perspective of the teacher. Sharing one's religious perspectives is appropriate as long as instructors are prepared to critically examine their own beliefs.

> Teachers with religious convictions should not be unduly burdened because of those convictions. Nor should they be uniquely benefitted. Religious convictions, if they are robust and go deep, are essential, not incidental, to who a person is and to what a person does.
>
> (Elshtain, 2002, p. 200)

A religious perspective is a part of the perspective any instructor brings to the classroom. Professors can represent a religion without advocating for that particular religion. A continuous conundrum for faculty is how to address religion and spirituality in curriculum and programming for students from a range of religious and spiritual backgrounds and viewpoints. These challenges can stem from ignorance and bias against non-Christian faiths. Issues of grades and instruction aside, students likely won't be happy, satisfied, and persistent if they are not happy inside the classroom. Issues related to religion are not limited to courses on religion. They may arise in history, political science, English, or other disciplines. An English course on religious texts, a political science course on Israel and Palestine, or a history course on Nazi Germany are likely to involve hot-button discussions that may be sensitive for all students but especially religious minorities.

Higher education's roots are in religion. Early American colleges were founded to train ministers, primarily. Though Harvard, Yale, and William and Mary were founded as Church affiliated, today they are not. "Most colonial colleges were founded to transmit and preserve the values, beliefs, traditions, and cultural heritage of their sponsoring denominational groups" (Kuh & Gonyea, 2006, p. 40). However, the tradition of religious education is still present.

Cherry, Deberg, and Porterfield (2001) identify three models for teaching religion in a college setting: advocacy, distanced objectivity, and the empathetic analytical (see Figure 4.1). In the advocacy model, instructors advocate for a particular religious tradition. Using distanced objectivity, instructors discourage judgment and use tools of literary criticism to evaluate religious text. Finally, the empathetic analytical model shows respect for all religions without advocating for one particular religion. The ideal model for college instructors of religion and related topics is the empathetic analytical model.

Advocacy	Distanced objectivity	Empathetic analytical
• Educators advocate for a particular religion and encourage student development in that tradition	• Instructors discourage judgment and use tools of literary criticism	• Instructors show respect for all religious traditions without advocating for a particular tradition

Figure 4.1 Three Models of Religious Education in the College Classroom (Cherry et al., 2001)

College instructors must distinguish from teaching about religion to teaching religion itself. Rhonda Hudstedt Jacobsen and Douglas Jacobsen describe the bias college instructors may struggle to combat:

All educators and researchers face a similar challenge. Each one of us is the product of our experiences, intellectual and cultural and spiritual. Despite years of training in religious studies (Douglas) and psychology (Rhonda), we recognize that we still have a host of internalized Protestant impulses that sometimes bubbled to the surface. By this, we mean especially Protestantism's emphasis on ideas more than practices and on the individual rather than the group. Of course, we are not alone in this Protestant bias, since Protestantism's broad cultural influence has shaped almost all of American higher education. This is even true at some self-defined "secular" liberal arts colleges where a Protestant ethos often prevails even though these schools have never been formally church-related.

(Nelson, 2012)

Here is an example of some classroom challenges experienced by a Muslim student related to diversity at a small, private, unaffiliated college.

There are certain faculty that are very wrapped up in whatever denomination of Christianity they identify with. And it's obvious, like I took an intro to religion class which is a requirement to take [here]. So I took Intro to Religion and I was the only Muslim in the class and it was an Intro to Religion class but all she [the instructor] seemed to know well was Christianity so all she presented was from a Christian lens. So when she presented Islam it was through a Christian lens and it was certain things that she said that wasn't – not that it wasn't correct but it wasn't clear, maybe certain people got the wrong perception of Islam from how she explained it so I raised my hand to assist her and that's probably how she found out

I was Muslim. At first she thanked me and then she said are you a Muslim and I said yes and she said oh so you're a Muslim so you can better explain certain things than me so she asked me to explain certain things and I did and she asked me what was the main difference that separated Christianity from Islam and that's when her facial expressions sort of let me know that she didn't agree with what I said.

(Anonymous, personal interview, 2013)

According to the account of this student, the professor exhibited signs of an advocacy model of religious teaching. She is unconsciously advocating for Christianity. All members of the campus community must acknowledge their own biases. That is one major step toward celebrating diversity. Religion professors may be most knowledgeable about Christianity even in courses that are about religion in general, not just Christianity. Instructors should keep the classroom a safe space for all students, regardless of students' religious identity.

The interview excerpt also demonstrates how some religious minorities may not immediately display or announce their identity as a religious minority. In the excerpt, the professor is not immediately aware that the student is Muslim. An introduction survey, such as the one below, administered on the first day of class, would have helped the professor be better informed about the constitution of her class and allow her to prepare discussions accordingly. Had the instructor known there was a Muslim student in the class, perhaps she would have taken steps to educate herself on Islam.

FACULTY CHALLENGES

According to Giles (2011), academic freedom not only involves the right of the professor to teach, but the right of a student to question and the right of the class to have a "free" and open discussion about a given topic. The question can and should be raised, "What happens when a professor's right to teach about a topic is violated? Such was the case of Douglas Giles, a Philosophy professor who has several years of experience teaching courses in both religion and philosophy. Giles was reprimanded by his then supervisor (department chair) for his pedagogical strategies regarding the Middle East and, in particular, his discussion of Israel and Palestine. Giles' approach was to treat groups with respect and dignity regardless of his personal feelings toward a specific group. He also allowed for his students to ask questions. The administrator of Giles was upset that Giles allowed a student to ask a question about Zionism in a World Religions course and he attempted to answer the question based on a religious studies perspective. The administrator made fervent remarks during her exchange with Giles, such as:

1. "How could you put a question about Zionism on a religion test? That is a totally inappropriate question."
2. "I hope you see that bringing politics into this is wrong. I don't think you can have any discussion of Zionism or the Palestinian issue other than in a political context" and it's "disrespectful to any Jews in the class to mention either of those."
3. "I hear you even allowed a Muslim to speak about their religion in class."
4. "Your job as a professor in a World Religions class is to tell them only the basic facts about each religion and nothing more."
5. "But you put this question into your test about the Israeli–Palestinian conflict. What disturbs me, Douglas, is that you act like the Palestinians have a side in this. They don't have a side! They are animals! They strap bombs to their bodies and blow up women and children! They are not civilized!"

Later, Giles was fired for his alleged "mishandling" of his World Religions class. He chose to speak out against this violation of his academic freedom, teamed up with a Philosophy Association Union, and was even offered his job back, which he refused. Giles mentioned the following important points of clarification in his article:

> Professors who teach world religions are charged to give an honest history of religions. It would be inappropriate for a world religions professor to abuse his or her position to advance an agenda that distorts history and forces students to acquiesce to a narrow and even bigoted ideology of any kind, whether promoting or condemning Zionism.... Respect is a virtue, and we owe it to all human beings. We should not engage in discussions or adopt textbooks that are willfully disrespectful to a group of people. But the supervisor was not asking for that basic human respect; she wanted to carve out an exceptional status for a particular group of people.
>
> (Giles, 2011, 223–224)

Giles' (2011) article represents an excellent discussion of the challenge professors may face in the discussion of controversial topics on religion. Professors themselves may also be members of religious minority faiths, which may affect how they are viewed on campus by higher education administrators, staff, and even their own students. Furthermore, professors in general may be more hesitant to discuss issues or religion and spirituality despite being cognizant of the importance of freedom of speech in higher education. Pedagogical practices in higher classrooms do not exist in a bubble but rather are shaped by larger social forces that in turn shape our ways of viewing the world and the importance we place on some subjects above others. It was argued that the event of September 11 highlighted our need to discuss issues of religious diversity on a larger scale (Rice, 2008). However, we would argue that this approach is more reactionary as we should not wait until tragedies occur to address problems. Muslim Americans have faced similar challenges in America to other visible racial, ethnic, religious minority groups in the country in regards to who speaks on behalf of such groups. There are a few historical insights which may have given rise to the placement of religion and spirituality in the classroom, which will be addressed further.

According to Rice (2008), modernization and secularization and the post-modern era had enormous effects on higher education in the United States. Modernization and secularization largely took place between 1957 and the 1960s. During this time period, funding had increased dramatically in the fields of science and technology, largely due to the "Cold War" between the former Soviet Union and America's quest to remain technologically and scientifically relevant, if not superior, to her foreign counterparts. Hence, existential higher education discussions were replaced in favor of more positivist or scientific approaches. In contrast, the post-modern era took place during the Vietnam War when the United States was entrenched in a huge social discourse surrounding the civil rights of racial and ethnic minorities in this country as well as the social standing of women. Although greater emphasis was placed on multiculturalism, it would take even longer for the words, experiences, scholarship, and contributions of scholars of color and women to be valued in their respective fields of study.

RELIGIOUS MINORITY PROFESSORS

Based on the research of Dugan (2007), Buddhist women professors have been actively involved in the stimulation of interfaith and interreligious dialogue on their respective college campuses. Some of these academics, including Diana Paul and Rita Ross, have been involved in the promotion of new understandings of women in Buddhist history and have advanced more gender neutral perceptions of women in Buddhist theology. Female academic Buddhologists have also been active in campus ministries which may have regular meditation circles. The presence of Buddhist faculty members and advisors of campus ministries may have positive effects on students of both Buddhist and non-Buddhist communities.

TEACHING PEDAGOGY IN RELIGIOUS STUDIES

Professors who teach religion-based courses in the classroom must make sure that they respect the diversity of their student's backgrounds and of the material. The first day of class is an opportunity to set expectations for class discussions on religious topics. Though personality differences may dictate how students choose to engage in class, the instructor can encourage the desired level of instruction by asking students about their expectations of a course on religion or about their conceptions of religious topics. Instructors may be surprised by what students may expect to cover in a course on religion. By asking students about their course expectations, instructors become aware of what students want to learn and can tailor the course accordingly. For example, students may advocate for a particular religious topic or perspective that the instructor had not planned to cover but is certainly willing to cover.

The importance of learning students' backgrounds and discussion preferences cannot be underestimated. Instructors must get to know students in order to have a productive semester. Icebreakers are typically "getting to know you" activities. However, an icebreaker in the college classroom can help students get acquainted with religious subject matter. Since names often have religious significance, instructors can encourage an opening discussion of religion by encouraging students to share any religious origin or meaning of their name. Conversely, instructors should be willing to share their religious background and faith traditions they adhere to, if any. The instructor should not allow students to assume he or she believes a certain way. By sharing about themselves, instructors develop a rapport with students in preparation for potentially difficult class discussions about religion. The information flow should be a two-way street between students and instructors.

Maley (2013) discusses how she uses icebreakers to shape how students approach the study of world religions.

Our icebreaker game hides a lesson in specific language: each student has to introduce himself by proclaiming something that makes him unique from the rest of the class. The catch is that if this unique trait is true of anyone else in our classroom community, the student has to think of something else. The underlying message, however, is that the more specific a student is in her language, the easier time she will have of being unique. If a student says he has a child, several others will raise their hands; however, if he says he has a 12-year old boy who plays the flute, likely this will not be true of others in the class. When the game is over, and we have all met, I point out the link to what we will be studying. I explain that in the typical way we discuss religion, we often use blanket, nonspecific statements, making claims about Christians or atheist or Hindus that fall easily into the kind of stereotypes that we would not tolerate if someone made those same claims about ethnicity or gender; so our first goal is to understand what we can about the groups we are studying while simultaneously recognizing that religion is only part of a full cultural understanding. For example, just because one is Christian does not mean she is antihomosexual, no matter what blanket statements are made in the media. As we study Christianity, we will see that some denominations are performing gay marriages, whereas others have decided to "love the sinner and hate the sin": two very different approaches from the same religion. Therefore, as we head into the study of religion, we need always think about specific language as the more precise we are in our discussions, the more critically we can study the religions we encounter.

(p. 63)

The following survey can help instructors to understand how the assessment of religious preferences of students could be utilized in an Introduction to Religious Studies or related course to further understand their knowledge and attitudes.

Religion 101 Survey

Dear Student, this survey will help me, your instructor, learn more about you and your expectations for the course. Completing this survey is optional and your answers will remain anonymous.

1. Do you adhere to a particular religion or spiritual/faith-based practice or belief system? If no, skip to question 4.
2. What religion or spiritual/faith-based practice do you adhere to?
3. If you selected Christianity, what denomination do you adhere to?
4. Were you raised, from childhood, in the tradition of a particular religion or spiritual practice?
5. If you answered yes to question 4, do you still adhere to the same religion?
6. Have you taken a religion course before?
7. Why are you taking this course?

    a. It's required.
    b. It fit my schedule.
    c. I'm interested in the subject, but this course isn't required for me.

8. What do you hope to learn from this course (free response limited to one sentence)?
9. What is your approach to discussing religion in class?

    a. I jump right in and voice my opinion regardless of whether it agrees with others.
    b. I listen first and offer my opinion whether it agrees with others or not.

  c. I listen and offer my opinion if others agree.

  d. I sit back and listen to the class and instructor, rarely offering my opinion.

College coursework should provide opportunities to strengthen writing. The following writing activities can be incorporated in a religion course. Students can keep a journal of their intellectual and emotional responses to religious topics discussed in class. In addition to helping students learn actively, students can use their journal responses to construct questions and comments for future discussions. Another activity is to have students craft an informational brochure of a religion or faith tradition different from their own, citing scripture and scholarly sources.

According to Nilson (2003), experiential activities such as role playing provide the opportunity for students to gain in-depth classroom experiences with religious diversity. Instructors can assign realistic, interfaith situations for students to act out representing different religions and faith traditions. Other experiential activities include a mock press conference and a panel discussion. During a mock press conference, a student acts as a religious scholar or clergy member and answers questions from classmates acting as journalists. A panel discussion could involve students as panel members representing various religions and faith traditions presenting on one topic, such as burial practices or marriage ceremony traditions.

Instructors of religion and related courses should give particular consideration to the texts utilized. Arroyo (2010) prioritizes the use of primary texts in religion courses.

> Primary sources give the class two important benefits. First, they put in the hands of the students verifiable proof that spiritual texts other than the one on their nightstand exist. Talking about these texts through secondary commentaries is insufficient: the students must see and read the Qur'an, the Gita, the Upanishads, the Tanak, the New Testament, and the Heart Sutra.
>
>   (p. 45)

Discussion on religious education and faith challenges in the college classroom are primarily Christian biased or centered. What is it like for students to have their religious beliefs challenged in the classroom? What happens when a course on religion includes students outside of Christianity? There can be disagreement or the challenge of beliefs within Christianity and outside of it. Differences beyond Christianity are where the real challenge lies for the instructor as far as maintaining a respectful and unbiased climate in the classroom. Faculty can be allies to religious minorities. Moreover, the classroom should be a safe space or at least a safer space. Faculty in religion or political science courses may need to change their pedagogy and assumptions about students to limit religious bias. No religious group is a monolith. Experiences within the same religion may differ by class, race, or nationality. Maley (2013) discusses how she encourages open discussions of world religions in the college classroom.

> In the World Religions classroom we spend our time introducing students to the ideas that (a) it is okay to talk about religion with people who may disagree with you, (b) there is a way to discuss religion in an academic setting that does indeed differ from a religious one, and (c) knowing information about other religions does not mean that you need to deny your own faith. Because most of your students have never encountered a course in religion in their academic career, we have to begin from scratch in a simultaneous process that tears down the typical insider and opinion-centered approaches students are used to with regard to religion while simultaneously developing in them a new lexicon of information that will allow them to have critical discussions about religion in the future.
>
> (p. 62)

Mays' point *b* deserves extra emphasis. Students may discuss religion in their respective places of worship and may be exposed to different religions through the media. However, discussing religion in an academic setting uses critical thinking skills not necessarily required in casual conversation or a religious setting. Critical thinking is a skill all college students need to develop and the religion classroom is an ideal setting for critical thinking skill development.

Frye (2007) offers four tips for instructors of religion and professors in other disciplines that may touch on religion.

1. Anticipate varying expectations from students. Try not to make assumptions or pre-judge. Administering a survey to learn more about students, their beliefs and their expectations for the course can help in this regard.
2. Instructors should model asking questions and including different beliefs. Leave the sarcasm and patronization out.
3. Develop an open and safe classroom climate. Instructors must set the tone early, not after a hostile exchange has already taken place. Learning can't take place if students, particularly religious minorities, don't trust the instructor.

Offering a religion class, even as a one-credit seminar, is an opportunity to introduce inclusion and interfaith programming. As colleges become more secularized, general education religion requirements are eliminated. In the interest of interfaith cooperation, eliminating religion requirements may be a mistake. Instead, institutions should consider revamping general religion courses to include contexts for religious pluralism and interfaith engagement. Maybe religion requirements don't need to be eliminated at schools that already had them. Harvard University dropped its religion requirement in 2007 amid concerns from faculty that the general education focus on religion was too strong (Bartlett, 2007). The elimination of religion requirements is one example of the secularization of higher education. Some believe that religion is for the uneducated masses and higher education should remain secular.

A one-credit worldview seminar would examine religion, spirituality, and belief systems from a diverse, interfaith perspective. First, the class would examine social theory as it relates to interfaith. Next, the course looks at the social history of the main religious minority groups in the United States. The course gives students the opportunity to acquire interfaith skills through an awareness of the various ways of seeing the world and the issues religious minorities and belief minorities face such as the experience of living as a non-Christian in the United States.

The following list was composed from various studies in the classroom in order to improve the quality of classroom instruction for teachers.

Curricular Development Tips (developed from the work of Drake, 1993)

1. Curriculum should be relevant to the course, free of partiality, and subject to change if needed. If at all possible, course materials should contain information from different racial, ethnic, religious and gender groups to provide a broader perspective. In the event that there is limited course information from various scholars, students should be told this.
2. A state of mind should be developed which allows teachers to accept differing opinions from their students.
3. Prospects for engagement, analytical thinking, and deciphering relevant topics should be infused within the course.
4. Create a positive attitude toward student learning outcomes.
5. Continue to educate yourself on the topic you teach and cultural differences.

Textbook Suggestions

*Note: Individual professors may elect to use other books, texts, or selected readings as primary.

Smart, Ninian. *Worldviews: Crosscultural Explorations of Human Beliefs*

Paden, William. *Interpreting the Sacred: Ways of Viewing Religion*

Bibliographical Suggestions

Scriptures:

Bible, Qur'an, Rg Veda, Buddhist Sutra, Tao Te Ching, etc.

Comparative Studies:

Armstrong, Karen, *A Case for God*

Doniger, Wendy, *Other People's Myths*

Eck, Diana, *A New Religious America*

Clooney, Frank, *Comparative Theology*

Kugel, James, *How to Read the Bible: Interpretation, Critical Methods and Modernity*

Michel, Thomas F. and Irfan Omar, eds., *A Christian View of Islam: Essays on Dialogue*

Pope John Paul II, Speech made at Israel's Holocaust Memorial March (2000) (online).

Pope Benedict XVI, "Faith, Reason and the University: Memories and Reflections"

Regensburg Address 2006; online: http://pontificateofpopebenedictxvi.blogspot.com/2008/08/regensburg-address-faith-reason-and.html (especially the first 16 paragraphs; read alongside the "Open Letter To Benedict XVI by 38 Leading Muslim Scholars and Leaders" and Benedict's official letter back to them).

Trible, Phyllis and Letty M. Russell, eds., *Hagar, Sarah, and Their Children: Jewish, Christian and Muslim Perspectives*

Vatican II documents such as: *Nostra aetate, Ad gentes, Dignitatis Humanae*

Non-Christian:

Al-Ghazali's Confessions

Raphael, Marc Lee, *Judaism in America*

Malcolm X *Autobiography*

Reps, Paul, *Zen Flesh Zen Bones*

Kehoe, Alice, *The Ghost Dance*

Wadud, Amina, *Qur'an and Woman*

Modern/Other:

Abraham, Susan and Elena Procario-Foley, *Frontiers in Catholic Feminist Theology*

Cone, James, *A Black Theology of Liberation* or *God of the Oppressed*

Copeland, M. Shawn, *Enfleshing Freedom*

Freud, Sigmund, *The Future of an Illusion*

Gonzalez, Michelle, *Created in God's Image*

King Jr., Martin Luther, *A Testament of Hope* (selections) (James Washington, ed.)

Juergensmeyer, Mark, *Terror in the Mind of God: The Global Rise of Religious Violence*

LaCugna, Catherine Mowry, ed., *Freeing Theology*

Niebuhr, H. Richard, *The Meaning of Revelation* or *The Responsible Self*

Niebuhr, Reinhold, *Moral Man and Immoral Society* or *The Nature and Destiny of Man*

Williams, Delores, *Sisters in the Wilderness*

Sample Course

Outline #2

Week	Topic
1	Basic concepts in the study of Religion
2–3	Basic concepts in Christianity and Judaism
4	Introduction to Mysticism
5	Comparative elements and methods – sacred time and space, pilgrimage
6–9	Religious experience (For example: conversion and religious narratives, such as Augustine, *Confessions* Malcolm X, *The Autobiography of Malcolm X*)
10–12	Myth (For example: Wendy Doniger, *Other People's Myths*)
13–14	Scripture and Interpretation (For example: James Kugel, *How to Read the Bible: Interpretation, Critical Methods and Modernity* Amina Wadud, *Qur'an and Woman*)

Figure 4.2 Sample Revised Theology Syllabus Template from Loyola University, Chicago

Source: www.luc.edu/media/lucedu/theology/pdfs/coresyllabi/Theo%20107%20Intro%20to%20Religious%20Studies.pdf).

1. Gandhi
2. Malcolm X
3. Moozlum
4. Roots
5. Prince Among Slaves
6. Betty and Coretta
7. Ali
8. Lost in Religion
9. Kumare
10. Beyond Our Differences
11. Pillars of Faith: Religions Around the World
12. Three Faiths, One God: Judaism, Christianity, Islam
13. Islam: Empire of Faith
14. The Message
15. The Buddha: The Story of Siddhartha
16. Elusive Peace: Israel and the Arabs
17. Judaism, Christianity and Islam: More in Common Than You Think
18. The Gates of Jerusalem: The History of the Holy City
19. Kingdom of Heaven
20. Jerusalem: Center of the World
21. Seven Years in Tibet
22. The Zen Mind
23. Baraka: A World Beyond Words
24. The Book of Negroes

Figure 4.3 DVD Listing Which May Spark Larger Discussions of Religious Pluralism in the Classroom

TEACHING ABOUT STEREOTYPING/CONTROVERSIAL ISSUES

In terms of discussions that promote anti-racist/anti-religious sentiment, stereotypical notions of groups should be confronted in the classroom. Students may be asked to anonymously write down on a piece of paper some dominant stereotypes about the religious group in question. It should be stated that, just like racial minority groups, religious minorities are also subject to overgeneralizations. For example, general discussions of Jews may focus on the Jewish political lobby as controlling American politics and the Israeli government's treatment of Palestinians in the occupied territories, with little discussion of Jewish resistance against the occupation (Milner & Spiegelman, 1992).

It should also be made clear that remarks which may be given the façade of anti-Zionist may in all actuality come across as anti-Semitic. American Jews have diverse origins, have a distinct culture, and constitute an ethnic and religious minority group. However, their voice is often left out of minority and ethnic studies curriculums in comparison to their ethnic counterparts. In particular, the historical contributions of Ashkenazi and Sephardic Jews have been absent from European centered curricula as well as multicultural curricula (Milner & Spiegelman, 1992).

Beyond the standard course evaluations used at most institutions, instructors of religion and related courses should conduct an additional evaluation to measure how the course addresses religious diversity and interfaith issues. The following is an example of a brief survey that can be used to evaluate religion courses.

Post-Course Evaluation Questions – Likert Scale

- As a religious minority, this course validated my experiences.
- As a Christian/member of the religious majority, I am more aware of religious minority experiences in the United States.
- This course is useful for students interested in careers involving interfaith work.
- During this course, I felt comfortable discussing my beliefs.
- During this course, I felt comfortable discussing beliefs different from my own.

RELIGIOUS STUDIES COURSE OFFERINGS AT THE NATION'S BEST UNIVERSITIES

According to the U.S. News and World Report (2015), out of a pool of 500, the top ten global universities include Harvard, MIT, UC Berkeley, Stanford, University of Oxford, University of Cambridge, California Institute of Technology, UCLA, University of Chicago, and Columbia University. Of the top ten, eight are located in the United States. The rankings were based on global and regional research reputations, the impact of citations, the number of Ph.D.s awarded, and international collaborations, among other research-related items. A selection of the spring 2015 undergraduate course offerings of the top three U.S. universities are listed in Table 4.1.

The course selections of the top three globally ranked U.S. universities shed much light onto the topic of the importance of rigorous curriculums which allow for many different voices. The array of courses offered at Harvard and The University of California at Berkeley suggest that religious diversity is taken seriously in order to be viewed as a top-ranking university. In contrast, MIT had a much smaller selection of such courses, which may be due to its focus on science, mathematics, and technological innovations. Other colleges and universities in America should take the lead in terms of the expansion of their course offerings to include special topics related to the nexus between history, politics, religion, and culture. American students should have the

Table 4.1 A Spotlight on Colleges and Universities with Course Offerings that Appeal to Religious Diversity on Campus

1. **Harvard University (Private Institution)**
   Relevant Majors/Minors
   African and African American Studies, Anthropology, Religion, General Education, History, Near Eastern Languages and Civilizations, Economics, and Philosophy

   Selected Courses
   African & African American Studies: African Religions, Indigenous Religious Traditions and Modernity, Seminar: Christianity, Identity, and Civil Society in Africa, Voodooizations and the Politics of Representation

   Religion: World Religions Face the Climate Crisis, Buddhism and Social Change, From Saint to Witch: Female Spirituality in the European Middle Ages, Religion and Public Health

   General Education: Religion in India: Texts and Traditions in a Complex Society, The Enlightenment, Freshmen Seminar: Beauty and Christianity

   Near Eastern Languages and Civilizations: Al-Ghazali: Theologian and Mystic, Knowledge and Authority in Muslim Societies, Introduction to Mesopotamian Religion, History of the Religion of Ancient Israel, Understanding Islam and Contemporary Muslim Societies

   History: An Introduction to Issues in American Indian Studies: Black Elk Speaks, Epidemiology: Religion and Public Health

   Anthropology: Religions of Latin America: Mexico, Peru, El Caribe, The Talking Dead: Archaeology of Death, Burials and Commemoration, Religion, Nation, and Government in Modern South Asia

   Philosophy: Saints, Heretics, and Atheists: An Historical Introduction to the Philosophy of Religion

   East Asian Languages and Civilizations: Introduction to the Study of East Asian Religions, Readings on Chinese Religions: Recent Scholarship on Chinese Buddhism and Daoism: Seminar, Sages, Saints, and Shamans: An Introduction to Korean Religions, The Study of East Asian Religions

   Economics: Religion and Political Economy, and Religion and the Rise of Capitalism

2. **MIT (Private Institution)**
   Relevant Majors/Minors
   Anthropology, History, and Philosophy

   Selected Courses
   Philosophy: Moral Problems and the Good Life, Moral Psychology, Ethics, Doing Right, Being, Thinking, Doing (or Not): Ethics in Your Life, Topics in Philosophy of Religion, and Topics in Moral Philosophy Global Studies and Languages: German and Jewish Responses to the Holocaust: Literature of Extremity and Responsibility

   Anthropology: Magic, Science and Religion, Dilemmas in Biomedical Ethics: Playing God or Doing Good?

   History: Palestine and the Arab-Israeli Conflict, Islam, the Middle East, and the West, Christianity in America, and Early Christianity

continued

83

Table 4.1 Continued

3. University of California at Berkeley (Public Institution)
Relevant Majors/Minors
East Asian Languages and Cultures, Anthropology, Celtic Studies, Chicano Studies, Arabic, Buddhist Studies, History, Celtic Studies, Chicano Studies, and Hebrew

Selected Courses
Anthropology: Religion and Anthropology, Seminars and Social and Cultural Anthropology: Religion

Arabic: Islamic Religious and Philosophical Texts in Arabic

Asian American Studies: Muslims in America, Islamophobia and Constructing Otherness, Religions of Asian America

Buddhist Studies: Introduction to the Study of Buddhism, Tibetan Buddhism, Japanese Buddhism, Buddhism in China, Buddhism on the Silk Road, Buddhism and the Environment, Buddhism in Contemporary Society, Zen Buddhism, Pure Land Buddhism, Tantric Traditions of Asia, Readings in Chinese Buddhist Texts, Introductory Readings in Japanese Buddhist Texts, Death, Dreams, and Visions in Tibetan Buddhism, Topics in the Study of Buddhism, Seminar in Tibetan Buddhism, Readings in Indian Buddhist Texts, Seminar in Buddhism and Buddhist Texts, Art and Archaeology of Buddhism

Celtic Studies: Celtic Christianity

Chicano Studies: Latina/o Philosophy and Religious Thought Chinese: Buddhism in China, Topics in Daoism, Readings in Chinese Buddhist Texts, Confucius and his Interpreters, Classics: Ancient Religion Comparative Literature: The Biblical Tradition in Western Literature Dutch: Anne Frank and After: Dutch Literature of the Holocaust in English Translation, English: The English Bible as Literature Gender and Women's Studies: Women in the Muslim and Arab Worlds

Hebrew: Post-Biblical Hebrew Texts, Elementary Biblical Hebrew, Biblical Hebrew Texts, The Art and Culture of the Talmud: Advanced Cultural Analysis, Advanced Biblical Hebrew Texts, Advanced Late Antique Hebrew Texts,

History: The Rise of Islamic Civilization 600–1200, History of Christianity to 1250, History of Christianity from 1250

Note: The list of courses related to religious diversity is not exhaustive and may only reflect the Spring 2015 course listings on the respective university websites and may not represent a comprehensive list of all classes taught at each university which encompasses religious diversity. Also, the current table primarily includes courses offered at the undergraduate level and does not include courses listed under the Harvard School of Divinity since it is a graduate program.

opportunity to study and discuss the plight of religious minority groups, but this is unlikely to happen if there are few, if any, course offerings.

When it comes to course offerings which appeal to religious diversity at private institutions, Harvard is at the top of the pack and for good reason. Eight relevant majors/minors were identified which offered courses in religious diversity. After a perusal of Harvard's spring 2015 course offerings, 27 courses were found which have a religion component. Of the 27 courses, several stand out as being exemplary unique offerings in terms of pedagogy:

World Religions Face the Climate Crisis, Freshman Seminar: Beauty and Christianity, Al-Ghazali: Theologian and Mystic, An Introduction to American Indian Studies: Black Elk Speaks, and From Saint to Witch: Female Spirituality in the European Middle Ages.

A Huffington Post article published in 2013 suggests that, despite popular thought, seminaries and schools of divinity are becoming increasingly transformative in terms of social engagement and change. The article was entitled "Seminaries that Change the World: A Growing List of Transitional Institutions for Transformational Times" and listed a selection of universities that were praised for producing students who were more socially engaged. Among them were both Ivy League universities, religiously affiliated and non-religiously affiliated schools such as: Princeton Theological Seminary, Yale Divinity School, Christian Theological Seminary, Austin Presbyterian Theological Seminary, Wesley Seminary, Vanderbilt Divinity School, and Columbia Theological Seminary (Meisel, 2013). In order to make it on the list, schools shared some of the following criteria: financial aid was given to students and an increased effort was made on the part of the school to reduce student debt, courses were offered which seek to incorporate both faith and service, and faculty, staff, and administrators supported a campus culture of engagement (Meisel, 2013).

CREATING AN OPEN CAMPUS DIALOGUE

In Chickering, Dalton, and Stamm's *Encouraging Authenticity and Spirituality in Higher Education* (2006), the authors make a strong plea for a more genuine and transcendent college campus of the near present and the future. The authors delineate between religion and spirituality in that they view religion as more dogmatic (external validations) but spirituality as more fluid and subject to internal validations. An institutional emphasis on the spiritual expansion of students may have major benefits not only for the student and their satisfaction but also for the university as it may reduce drop-outs/longer matriculations. Our concern is not so much with spirituality but with authenticity as we believe it is easier to be authentic than spiritual. While both may be realistic goals, perhaps authenticity has a higher possibility of being achieved as it pertains to a "consistency" in word and action. In the place of spirituality, we advocate the encouragement of being a compassionate student. Nonetheless, we agree that both are sorely needed in our seemingly narcissistic society (see Twenge & Campbell, 2009).

Chapter 6 discusses religious pluralism in the context of college courses. The freshman seminar or orientation is an opportunity to introduce religious diversity and interfaith engagement to entering students. College instructors must acknowledge their own religious beliefs and biases in order to connect with religious minority students, though colleges are increasingly secularizing by eliminating a general education religion requirement. However, courses in a religion major, history, English, and political science have the potential to raise controversial religious discussions in the classroom. The instructor must keep the classroom a safe space for students of any religious background through these discussions.

DISCUSSION QUESTIONS

1. What are the benefits of classrooms being welcoming spaces for religious minorities?
2. How might a professor's personal bias affect their students in general? In contrast, how might a professor's personal religious bias affect their religious minority students?
3. What actions should a professor take to ensure that they minimize bias in the classroom?
4. What steps should a student take (if any) if they feel that they are being marginalized or ignored in a classroom because of their religious beliefs?
5. Why is it important that professors and students maintain an open and respectful dialogue?
6. Describe what a classroom that is a "safe space" looks like. In other words, what are its characteristics?
7. Should senior administrators (e.g., deans, department chairs, provosts, university presidents) be involved in the curricular selection of faculty who teach religious studies courses?
8. At the nation's top universities, which course offerings would you be interested in taking?
9. Are you surprised that seminaries are now changing their reputation and becoming promoters of social activism?

REFERENCES

Arroyo, A. (2010). It's not a colorless classroom: Teaching religion online to black college students using transformative postmodern pedagogy. *Teaching Theology and Religion, 13*(1), 35–50.

Bartlett, T. (2007). Harvard drops religion requirement. *The Chronicle of Higher Education, 53*(18).

Bowman, N.A., & Small, J.L. (2013). The experiences and spiritual growth of religiously privileged and religiously marginalized college students. In A. Bryant Rockenbach & M. Mayhew (eds) *Spirituality in College Students' Lives*. New York, NY: Routledge.

Cherry, C., DeBerg, B.A., & Porterfield, A. (2001). *Religion on Campus: What Religion Really Means to Today's Undergraduates*. Chapel Hill, NC: University of North Carolina Press.

Chickering, A.W., Dalton, J.C., & Stamm, L. (2006). *Encouraging Authenticity and Spirituality in Higher Education*. San Francisco, CA: Jossey-Bass.

Drake, D.D. (1993). Student diversity: Implications for classroom teachers. *The Clearing House, 66*(5), 264–266.

Dugan, K. (2007). Buddhist women and interfaith work in the United States. *Buddhist-Christian Studies, 27*, 31–50.

Elshtain, J. (2002). Religion and American democracy. *Religion, Politics, and the American Experience: Reflections on Religion and American Public Life*, 16–26.

Frye, S. (2007). Religious education and faith challenges in the college classroom. *Adult Learning, 18*(1), 12–14.

Giles, D. (2011). A case of forbidding academic engagement of Muslim and Jewish beliefs about the holy land. *Arab Studies Quarterly, 33*(3/4), 217–227.

Kuh, G.D., & Gonyea, R.M. (2006). Spirituality, liberal learning and college student engagement. *Liberal Education, 92*(1), 40–47.

Maley, M. (2013). Loving all your neighbors: Why community colleges need the academic study of religion. *New Directions for Community Colleges, 163*, 61–68.

Meisel, W. (2013, November 11). Seminaries that change the world: A growing list of transitional institutions for transformational times, *Huffington Post*. Retrieved from www.huffingtonpost.com/wayne-meisel/seminaries-that-change-th_b_4256 358.html.

Milner, J., & Spiegelman, D. (1992). Carrying it on: A report from the New Jewish Agenda Conference on Organizing against Racism and Anti-Semitism. *Bridges, 3*(1), 138–147.

Nelson, L. (2012, October 25) No longer invisible. *Inside Higher Ed*. Retrieved from www.insidehighered.com/news/2012/10/25/book-argues-colleges-should-do-better-job-engaging-religion.

Nilson, L. (2003). *Teaching at its Best: A Research-Based Resource for College Instructors*. San Francisco, CA: Anker.

Pew Forum on Religion and Public Life. (2010). *U.S. Religious Knowledge Survey*. Retrieved from: www.pewforum.org/2010/09/28/u-s-religious-knowledge-survey/.

Rice, R.E. (2008). Religious diversity and the making of meaning: Implications for the classroom. *Diversity and Democracy, 11*(1), 1–19.

Twenge, J.M., & Campbell, W.K. (2009). *The Narcissism Epidemic: Living in the Age of Entitlement*. New York, NY: Simon & Schuster.

U.S. News and World Report. (2015). *Best Global Universities Rankings*. Retrieved from www.usnews.com/education/best-global-universities/rankings.

FURTHER READING

Browne-Glaude, W. (2008). *Doing Diversity in Higher Education: Faculty Leaders Share Challenges and Strategies*. Rutgers, NJ: Rutgers University Press.

Calderon, J.Z., & Eisman, G. (2007). *Race, Poverty, and Social Justice: Multidisciplinary Perspectives Through Service Learning*. Sterling, VA: Stylus Publishing.

Hickman, R. (2004). Teaching art to Muslim students. *Visual Arts Research, 30*(2), 55–61.

McCarthy, K. (2007). *Interfaith Encounters in America*. Rutgers, NJ: Rutgers University Press.

Chapter 5

Campus Environment and Accommodations

According to Kazanjian, Keen, and Laurence (2010), "One dilemma that persists in higher education is the place of religion in college and university education and the challenges and opportunities posed by increasing religious diversity on campuses nationwide." This chapter will confront the challenges posed by increasing religious diversity on college campuses by addressing what religious minority students need to comfortably practice their faith on campus. Specifically discussed will be the availability of interfaith prayer/meditation rooms, kosher, halal, and/or vegetarian dietary offerings, headgear regulations, and interfaith/chaplain services. Consideration of holidays outside of the Christian tradition when creating the academic calendar, housing options for religious minorities, recruitment, and other accommodation issues will also be discussed in this chapter.

In March 2015, the New York City public schools announced that, beginning with the 2015–2016 school year, they would close in observance of Eid-ul-Fitr and Eid-ul-Adha, the two major Islamic holidays. This move is a major accommodation for Muslims in the New York City public school system and just one example of the changes encouraged by religious pluralism in the United States. The New York City department of education is the largest school district in the country. Rosh Hashanah is another religious minority (Jewish) holiday observed by the school system. Accommodations such as holiday observances eliminate the need for students and families to choose between education and faith. How can colleges make similar accommodations?

Institutions with a large percentage of religious minorities of a particular faith may opt to close for a particular holiday. If closing is not feasible for a smaller minority of students, a campus memorandum announcing the holiday and what the holiday is celebrating can be sent around allowing students and employees to be excused from class and work responsibilities. The announcement or memorandum serves as a notice to excuse students and employees as well as to educate the larger campus community about the significance of the holiday. This way the holiday is acknowledged on campus without the burden on the student to submit an excuse for missing class.

The religious diversity in the United States calls for a religiously responsive approach to meeting the needs of religious minority students. A religiously responsive approach can be modeled after a culturally responsive approach. However, the term "culturally" is not exactly relevant to issues of religions, faith, belief, and spirituality, or lack thereof. Student affairs practitioners that use religiously responsive practices hold high expectations for student engagement, value the religious resources of students, and encourage sociopolitical awareness of all students, but especially religious minority students. There is a connection between a student's identity and their faith. Religion is an aspect of student culture that is often overlooked (Dallavis, 2011). Student affairs practitioners must consider spiritual and religious life as a dimension of student engagement. If students' beliefs aren't engaged religiously, spiritually, or otherwise, student engagement is lacking a critical element. Student engagement is most effective when factors such as prior experiences, the external community, cultural background, and religious identity are considered in its implementation. Also, student affairs practitioners should view religious diversity as a cultural asset to the institution as well as another aspect of student identity that needs to be addressed by student services and programming. In essence, student affairs practitioners must become students of minority faiths and beliefs in order to understand and engage religious minority students.

Campus accommodations should encourage success inside and outside of the classroom. For students, life on campus is very different from life at home. At home, religious minority students have family and friends with whom to practice religious rituals. Living on campus may leave a void for religious minority students who are used to completing religious rituals with family and friends or a congregation. The main objective of providing these accommodations is to help students adhere to their religion as they persist toward degree completion.

Culturally responsive approaches in higher education have been used to address race issues. In regards to religion, the term religiously responsive is more appropriate than culturally responsive. Though they are often confused, religion and culture are not the same. Since culture and religion are not one and the same, and students could have the same culture but practice different faiths, this term is more relevant to the challenges student affairs practitioners must overcome.

Religiously responsive practices also challenge ideas from the dominant religion about what it means to be engaged. Students have to engage the way they want to, not how student affairs professionals want them to. Also, student affairs professionals and faculty need to engage in self-reflective practice to explore their own religious backgrounds and assumptions and how these behaviors and assumptions influence their behavior toward religious minorities.

RELIGION AND THE LAW IN HIGHER EDUCATION

A discussion of religion in higher education must include what the law dictates on the subject. The establishment clause of the First Amendment requires public institutions to maintain religious neutrality. In other words, public institutions cannot support one religion over another or even support religion over secularism. Specifically, public colleges cannot employ an official prayer (*Engel* v. *Vitale*, 1962) The First Amendment also prohibits government from establishing religion and protects the practice of religion from government influence. The legal requirement of religious neutrality does not mean public institutions must prohibit religious activity at university-sponsored events. Kaplin and Lee (2007) highlight the limits of religious neutrality on college campuses:

> if a rigidly observed policy of neutrality would discriminate against campus organizations with religious purposes or impinge on an individual's right to freedom of speech or free exercise of religion, the institution may be required to allow some religion on campus.
>
> (p. 43)

The right to conduct religious activities on public college campuses was upheld in *Widmar* v. *Vincent* (1981), a U.S. Supreme Court case involving *Cornerstone*, a Christian organization, at the University of Missouri at Kansas City. Cornerstone was a campus-sponsored organization that previously had permission to hold meetings in campus facilities and was prohibited from continuing to do so based on a campus regulation prohibiting the use of campus facilities for religious worship. The court determined that right of this religious organization to meet was upheld by the First Amendment's free speech clause because campus facilities are considered a public forum, since they are open for student use. The court also opined in this decision that the First Amendment establishment clause (prohibiting the establishment of religion) is not violated wherever students conduct religious activities in campus facilities in which they normally have access.

Rosenberger v. *Rector and Visitors of the University of Virginia* (1995) addressed campus religious organizations' eligibility for funding from mandatory student activity fees. Wide Awake Productions (WAP) was a recognized organization on campus and allowed to use university facilities. However,

WAP was not allowed to receive funding from mandatory student activity fees because it was a religious organization. Specifically, WAP's mission included the expression of religious views. Also, WAP published a newsletter of articles presenting religious perspectives. Student organizations used student activities by submitting bills from third-party vendors. Therefore, funds were not sent directly to the organization. The U.S. Supreme Court reversed the district and appellate court's judgments and ruled in favor of WAP. The court opined that, since the student activity fee was mandatory for students, funds from those fees were essentially a public forum. To restrict use of those fees by religious speech or perspective was to violate the free speech clause of the First Amendment.

The U.S. Supreme Court has a record of rejecting claims of religious establishment at public universities. In *Tanford* v. *Brand* (1997), the U.S. Court of Appeals for the Seventh Circuit affirmed Indiana University's tradition of nonsectarian invocations and benedictions during commencement exercises. In the instance of a commencement ceremony, the court opined that the purpose of an invocation or benediction was to solemnize an important occasion, not to spread religious teachings. Commencement attendance was not required, nor was there a penalty imposed on students for not attending. Moreover, approximately a third of Indiana's graduating students opted to skip the commencement exercises. Historically, Indiana University invited representatives from a range of denominations and faiths to complete the invocation and benediction.

In *Chaudhuri* v. *Tennessee* (1997), a Hindu professor claimed that Tennessee State University's (TSU) use of prayer during university functions constituted the establishment of religion. In addition to graduation ceremonies, prayers were conducted during faculty meetings, guest lectures, and other campus events at Tennessee State. A moment of silence was substituted for a prayer after the lawsuit was filed. The plaintiff challenged the use of a moment of silence as well. Again, the court opined that the purpose of a prayer in these settings was to dignify a particular occasion, not to conduct religious worship. Moreover, attendance at functions where prayers or a moment of silence was offered was not mandatory, nor was there any risk of indoctrination from the prayers.

In *Lee* v. *Weisman* (1992), the U.S. Supreme Court ruled in favor of a family objecting to a prayer during a high school graduation ceremony. The school principal gave the selected religious official, a Rabbi, a pamphlet on composing prayers for civic occasions. The court interpreted this action as establishment of religion, even though the prayer offered was nonsectarian in nature. Also, the court opined that the peer pressure and expectation of grade school students to participate in the prayer by standing and the social significance of high school graduation attendance amounted to coercion to participate in the prayer. A third of graduating students opting to miss commencement exercises at a large, public university is not out of the ordinary. Contrarily, a third of graduating students opting to miss a high school graduation is odd, to say the least. To the U.S. Supreme Court, a grade school graduation and a college graduation do not hold the same weight in regards to prayer.

Private institutions are not legally bound to maintain religious neutrality. Moreover, the establishment and free exercise clauses that protect students' religious activities on public campuses also protect the rights of private colleges to support a particular religion or denomination (Kaplin & Lee, 2007). The aforementioned court rulings are an abridgement of what is allowed by law regarding students and religion on college campuses. When considering the inclusion of religious minorities, colleges and universities may want to go beyond what the law requires to ensure that students of all worldviews are included and satisfied.

RELIGIOUS PRIVILEGE

Fried (2007) provides a definition for religious privilege: "Religious privilege exists where the beliefs, practices and world view of one dominant group dominates and is accepted, almost unconsciously, by members of the dominant group, marginalizing all other beliefs" (Fried, 2007, p. 3). Religious privilege impacts aspects of campus life, such as the academic calendar, dining options, and the allocation of space (Kocet & Stewart, 2011). Even public or nonsectarian institutions implement policies, schedules, or programming that is biased toward the religious majority. Some examples of this are chapels on campuses that are not religiously affiliated and campus closure on Good Friday and/or Easter Monday, in addition to the convenience of the semester break coinciding with Christmas. While Christians do enjoy a certain amount of privilege, as discussed throughout the book, certain denominations do not enjoy the same level of privilege because larger Christian denominations do not view smaller groups, such as Seventh Day Adventists and the Church of Jesus Christ of Latter-Day Saints, as true Christians (Schlosser, 2003). Here is an abbreviated list of Christian privileges adapted from McIntosh (1989) and Schlosser (2003):

- I can be sure to hear music on the radio and watch specials on television that celebrate the holiday of my religion.
- I can assume that I will not have to work or go to school on my significant religious holidays.
- I can be sure that when told about the history of civilization, I am shown people of my religion who made it what it is.

- I do not need to worry about the ramifications of disclosing my religious identity to others.
- I can be sure that when my children make holiday crafts, they will bring home artistic symbols of the Christian religion.
- I am never asked to speak for all the people of my religious group.
- I can, if I wish, arrange to be in the company of people of my religion most of the time.
- I can, if I wish to identify myself, safely identify as Christian without fear of repercussions or prejudice because of my religious identity.
- I can buy foods from major grocery stores and restaurants that meet the dietary guidelines of my religion.
- I can travel and be sure to find a comparable place of worship when away from my home.
- I can be sure that people are knowledgeable about the holidays of my religion and will greet me with the appropriate holiday greeting.

Ask yourself the next time you automatically wish a Jewish person Merry Christmas or Happy Easter, or when you are about to send a Christmas card, whether the person would truly welcome the gesture, or whether you might be imposing your traditions and values on that person.

(Blumenfeld & Klein, 2009, p. 37)

If you truly wish to offer a benevolent greeting, it is appropriate to act on that urge. However, consider the fact that everyone is not Christian. Or consider what a reciprocal greeting might look like from a religious minority holiday (Happy Hanukkah, Ramadan Mubarak, etc.). Therefore, everyone may not receive your card or greeting in the spirit in which it is given. This conundrum is an opportunity for mainline Protestants and those in the religious majority to dialogue about holiday celebrations.

Religious faith and observance, in its varying degrees, can be divisive. Even for those who follow the same religion, the perception that one is more religious than the other can create an "us versus them" mentality. Students with varying degrees of religious faith and practice can learn from one another, whether they follow the same religious faith or not. Appropriate campus culture and interfaith programming can bridge the gap between different faiths and levels of adherence.

Before religious minorities can be accommodated, an assessment of what these students need to comfortably practice their faith on campus must occur. Campus assessments are discussed in depth in Chapter 3. Larger cities and urban centers may have less of a demand for religious minority accommodation. Students in urban centers, particularly where the college or university has good relations with the external community, may have more options for religious accommodation. However, the concerns of religious minority students are equally important to urban, suburban, and rural campuses.

There is disagreement over the use and meaning of the word *interfaith*. The term *interfaith* can have negative connotations. *Interfaith* refers to interactions between persons who adhere to different faiths. These interactions could be one directional, most likely emanating from the dominant religion to minority religions. Interfaith could also mean one, dominant religion interacting with one minority religion. Where there are two, one will be dominant. Separate is usually not equal. Opponents of the term *interfaith* believe the term *multifaith* refers to multiple religions interacting equally. Sorrentino (2010) prefers the term *multifaith* over *interfaith*, claiming that *multifaith* places more emphasis on differences and similarities, while *interfaith* focuses more on commonalities only.

Conversely, the term *interfaith* is also preferred over *multifaith* by some interfaith activists. The blog *One Baha'i's Approach* explains the preference for *interfaith* over *multifaith*:

> When you interlock your fingers, you are taking your two hands and mingling the fingers together. The implication is that there are two separate things working very closely, and in unison. When I think of the ideal behind this movement, the interfaith movement, this is what I envision. Multitasking, on the other hand ... is when you use two separate hands to do two separate tasks. They are not working together, nor are they necessarily united. They are working separately from each other.

PLANNING AN INTERFAITH EVENT

Before implementing an interfaith curriculum, campuses who have executed little in the way of religious diversity may want to begin by hosting a single interfaith program or event. Sorrentino (2010) outlines the necessary elements of putting together a multifaith or interfaith gathering. Of course, planning efforts for an interfaith/multifaith event should be led by a religiously diverse team. The prospective event should not replace worship, service, or rituals of any particular religion. Terminology and descriptors related to the event should be general, secular, or not applicable only to a single religion or belief. Artistic expressions such as music and dance should be carefully considered. Selected speakers should use language that is comprehensible to a religiously diverse audience. Considerations for multifaith events are particularly important when a tragedy or celebration impacts the entire campus community. Finally, Sorrentino's RAM (Respectful, Authentic, and Meaningful) principles are an evaluation tool for campus multifaith event planners. Multifaith events should be respectful to the beliefs of others while being authentic to one's own tradition, and include meaningful interreligious interaction. Figure 5.1 shows a process for planning a multifaith event.

RESOURCE ALLOCATION

All spiritual and religious groups should have equal opportunity to use campus resources. When multicultural or diversity affairs are discussed on college campuses, the discussion is usually centered on race, gender, or sexual orientation. As such, focus on religion is relatively new and unfamiliar territory. Is it easier to confront racism, sexism, homophobia, and other "isms" than it is religious discrimination? Are faith, spirituality, and religion an unfamiliar beast for student affairs practitioners to tackle? Student affairs practitioners confront the answers to these questions while attempting to create interfaith programs and religious inclusivity on college campuses. The author conjectures that student affairs practitioners are more likely to be under-informed about non-Christian religions, whereas race and gender issues are more comfortable territory. Bowman and Small (2013) speak to the challenges of addressing religion and spirituality at public and religiously affiliated institutions.

> Practitioners and administrators at public institutions may not feel comfortable being involved in spirituality or religiosity in any manner, and those at faith-based institutions may be inclined to focus on students with a particular religious affiliation or set of beliefs. Taken together, this leads to an overall blindness to the needs of double religious minorities during their college years, no matter the institutional type.
>
> (Bowman & Small, 2013, p. 31)

Religion forces students and practitioners to evaluate their religious beliefs and biases in a way that race does not. An individual can choose their faith and choose to practice and worship as they please. Race, though a social

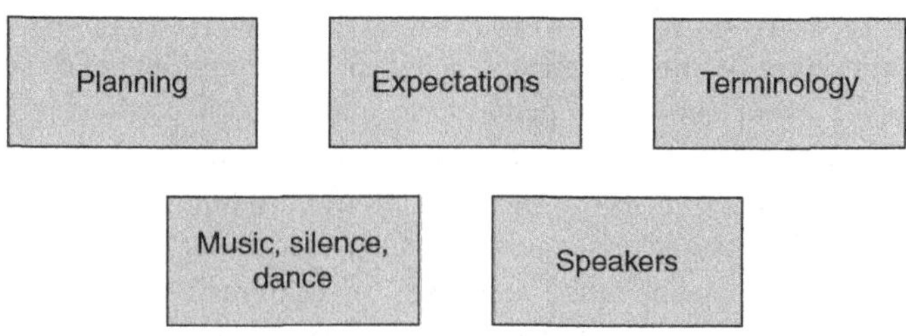

Figure 5.1 Sorrentino's (2010) Process for Planning a Multifaith Event

construction, is more concrete. Race and religion contribute different but important aspects to a person's identity. Religion, with the exception of religious clothing, does not make one hyper-visible in the way that race can.

Religious attire is a venue of religious expression that can also make religious adherents hyper-visible. From the clerical collar to the yarmulke to the niqab, religious adherents can be identified by the clothing they choose to wear. Any attire can speak volumes about an individual's culture and values, and religious attire is no different.

How does a campus implement interfaith programming and create a religiously inclusive campus climate? How should campuses accommodate religious minorities and educate the campus community about religions and spiritual practices outside of Christianity? Student affairs practitioners should use a sociopolitical approach to implement interfaith programming and accommodations. A sociopolitical approach considers power, oppression, and privilege while creating a religiously inclusive campus community (Clark, 2003). Accommodations are more meaningful when they are accompanied by programming that educates the campus community on the history and origins of minority religions and Christian privilege.

College administrators are often too cautious about sponsoring any form of religious expression (Moran, Roberts, Tobin, & Harvey, 2008). The separation of church and state in the United States does not mean that colleges cannot support religious expression, which is different from proselytizing. College administrators also fear litigation related to religious expression. "The fear of being sued can cause us to reduce our relationships to a transactional level" (Allen & Kellom, 2001, p. 50). The fear of excluding students can negatively impact the actions of student affairs practitioners and administrators. For example, some institutions fear the perceived exclusion of other religious groups by the provision of a prayer room requested by one group. Na'im (pseudonym), a Muslim, discusses the response from his private, religiously unaffiliated college when a prayer room was requested:

[The response] it's been if we have a prayer room for Muslims then we have to do this and we have to do that. Does it have to be called a Muslim prayer room? I'm like we don't care what it's called as long as we have a place to go to establish *salat* [prayer] on campus. They say we have to call it something else that is more encompassing of other religions and we don't have a problem with that. They try to say we have to find a space but there is plenty of room, there might be too much actually, but there is plenty of space on campus that we could use as a prayer room.

(Anonymous, personal communication, July 13, 2013)

MISSION AND STRATEGIC PLAN

An institution's mission and campus culture can impact student spirituality and learning outcomes (Kuh & Gonyea, 2006). This is one reason why an institution's mission is important to religious diversity. All students, regardless of their faith, should have the opportunity to have their spirituality enhanced during their college experience, if they so desire. Accommodation of religious minorities should not be incidental. Schools should first review their missions to assess how religious diversity is addressed. Before institutions can attempt to accommodate religious minorities, vision statements, mission statements, and diversity strategic plans should address religious diversity. An institution's mission should be reflected through the campus environment. A mission provides the background for a strategic plan to proactively meet the needs of religious minorities. Without a mission and/or strategic plan that addresses religious diversity, meeting the needs of religious minorities may become a haphazard afterthought or a reaction to conflict. Meredith College, a Baptist-affiliated women's college in North Carolina, is an example of one institution that addresses religious diversity in its mission through its core values statement. Despite its Baptist affiliation, Meredith College emphasizes the importance of religious diversity. Meredith College's mission statement and core values are shown in Figure 5.2. Strategic plans are discussed in depth in Chapter 3.

Accommodations can be tangible or physical, such as buildings, rooms, calendar adjustments, meals, etc. Accommodations can also be cultural, such as adjusting prayer and devotional speeches during campus events to be more religiously inclusive. What are the obligations of colleges in accommodating religious minorities? From the first day a religious minority student steps on campus, he or she may have concerns that a Christian will not have. This new religious minority student may wonder: Will I struggle to share a living space with a person of a different faith? Will the campus dining options meet my needs? What if I have a test that falls on a religious holiday that I observe?

DINING OPTIONS

College campuses, particularly very large campuses, offer a plethora of dining options. However, these options may still leave something to be desired for the most devout religious minority students.

> While Catholic students are virtually certain to find meatless entrees on Fridays, it is not a foregone conclusion that institutional dining halls follow kosher practices for the orthodox Jewish students on campus. Nor is it a certainty that Muslim students will find a dining hall open for iftar.
>
> (Seifert, 2007)

Retrieved from: http://www.meredith.edu/about_meredith/mission_and_values

Mission Statement

Meredith College, grounded in the liberal arts and committed to professional preparation, educates and inspires students to live with integrity and provide leadership for the needs, opportunities and challenges of society.

Vision

Meredith College is respected nationally as a vibrant learning environment in which students enhance their strengths, broaden their perspectives, and prepare for lives of impact and distinction.

Values

The Meredith College community is dedicated to core values drawn from Meredith's mission and heritage, including its founding as a women's college by North Carolina Baptists.

These values serve as the foundation for our programs, our interactions with each other and our outreach beyond the campus:

- Integrity… upholding high standards of truth and personal honor;
- Intellectual freedom… fostering a spirit of openness and inquiry, and respecting a range of perspectives and voices;
- Academic excellence… promoting scholarship, innovation, curiosity, intellectual challenge, hard work, and lifelong learning;
- Responsible global citizenship… contributing positive change through ethical leadership and civic engagement;
- Personal development… seeking intellectual, personal, and spiritual growth through structured and individual learning and experience;
- Religious diversity… avowing the College's Christian heritage while respecting all faiths and spiritual beliefs; and
- Relevance… meeting society's needs by educating students in programs that prepare them for the future.

Figure 5.2 Meredith College Core Values and Mission Statement

If the food is not kosher, Jewish students are forced to select a vegetarian meal. In a study of 1,087 Jewish students at eight colleges in the United States, Kadushin and Tighe (2008) found that the lack of kosher dining facilities presented challenges to Jewish students.

Catered events and receptions on campus may present an additional challenge. If the staff in charge of ordering food for an event is unknowledgeable about the dietary requirements of religious minorities, he or she may order a meal where pork is the only option, such as pepperoni pizza or salami submarine sandwiches. A Muslim student at a public, rural university describes his campus dining experiences:

> What sometimes would happen is that there'd be like nothing but pork or like bologna, salami, ham, and I would kind of be like, I'll just hang out, no worries. And honestly, you know what? All other certain people would react the same way that I did. I kind of, the way I went about it was, you know, people don't know that I don't eat pork. I have to go out and teach them. So it's like I could easily, just easily get really up in arms about it, be like what the heck, this is really, really dumb, I don't know why they don't see this. But I have to understand as a sociology major that, you know, sometimes people, the exposure that they get is different in different parts of the world. So I can't get upset at them for not knowing. We addressed it with student services or whoever the coordinating person at the event was. To just be mindful of those who don't eat pork. We want to make sure that everybody has a place at the table.
>
> (Anonymous, personal communication, July 1, 2013)

The rural location of the university is important because it means the availability of food off campus is limited. Also, this student did not have a car to travel through the rural area to seek out food options. Dining availability can become an issue during Ramadan, when Muslims do not eat or drink from sun up to sun down (Ali & Bagheri, 2009). Dining hall schedules may need to be adjusted or separate accommodations made for Muslim students. Administrators should keep in mind that, since Islamic holidays follow the lunar calendar, Ramadan moves 10 days earlier every year. Another Muslim student at a private, religiously unaffiliated institution discusses the cafeteria options on his campus:

> I remember when I came in freshman year it was like two weeks of Ramadan left so that's why it's a real problem during Ramadan. We can't eat during the day. At the time, the cafe is closed so we had to go in and get some food to carry back to the room. It has gotten better since freshman year but I do remember freshman year sometimes there would be pork in everything and there wouldn't be much for me to choose from in the cafeteria to eat because it was like swine in almost everything but it has gotten better. There has been changes a little bit but it was horrible freshman year.
>
> (Anonymous personal communication, July 13, 2013)

PRAYER/MEDITATION ROOMS

Social relations guide the allocation of space on a college campus. On many campuses, the allocation of worship space remains traditional, while other aspects of the campus plant are modernized. The earliest colleges and universities in the United States were modeled after British institutions, complete with affiliation and sponsorship from a church or Christian entity. A primary mission of these early institutions was to train ministers (Geiger, 2011). Today, many of those early institutions have loosened or completely severed ties with the church, though relics from that era remain on their campuses. For many universities today, the campus plant is not complete without a chapel.

Prayer rooms are probably the most requested accommodation from religious minorities on college campuses. While prayer rooms are a significant accommodation, they will never be on the same level of sacredness as a chapel or a space specifically created for religious worship, such as a synagogue or mosque. "Having a physical space in which to practice their religion can also be an area in which Christian students have privilege" (Seifert, 2007, p. 13). Nevertheless, prayer rooms on campus are important for more than physical accommodations.

Prayer rooms represent a place where religious minorities are not the *other* as they might be in the classroom, the cafeteria, or elsewhere on campus (Gilliat-Ray, 2000). Also, providing a prayer room signals recognition as a group by a college administration instead of an individual tolerance of difference. A shared prayer room may not be as meaningful or sacred as an historic chapel but it is a tangible sign of efforts to accommodate religious minorities. Prayer or meditation rooms will appeal to Muslim students in particular, whether they live on or off campus, since the five daily prayers occur during the day when they are away from home or mosque. An interfaith space also accommodates Atheist or Agnostic students who want a quiet place to meditate and reflect. Jews also attend a morning Minyan or public prayer service which would be made easier with a room on campus to do so (Kadushin & Tighe, 2008).

Religious diversity must be embraced through architectural spaces on campus, as well as programming and staffing. These spaces demonstrate a commitment to the spiritual life of a religiously diverse group of students. Student affairs administrators and practitioners should not wait until the demand for prayer room accommodations are overwhelming or contentious. Investments in accommodating religious minority students will yield returns in the form of increased student satisfaction and persistence.

The following guidelines should be followed to establish and maintain a prayer/meditation room. The prayer room should be situated near a restroom for students who would like to perform ablution before praying or meditating. Also, marketing is needed to let students know that the room exists. A grand opening event will also help publicize the availability of the room. A room divider or curtain is also useful in an interfaith prayer space for students who wish to separate from the opposite sex while praying. Prohibiting food and beverages will help keep the prayer room clean. Also, shoes should not be worn in the room to keep it clean for those who pray without shoes. Therefore, a shoe rack will be necessary to hold shoes. Your campus should determine if the room will hold meetings in the space. Meetings could be distracting to students who are praying and meditating. A small budget should be provided for the maintenance of the room.

Institutions have expanded the use of their chapel to include faiths other than Christianity. There are conflicting views on retrofitting chapels for interfaith purposes. Chapels were designed for Christian worship and rituals. As such, retrofitting them for an interfaith prayer room is viewed by some as inappropriate. Gilliat-Ray (2000) quoted a chaplain as saying, "the chapel is designed, fitted, and used for Christian worship. It would be strange to conceal the traces of its being inhabited in this way. Places of worship are identity-shaping" (p. 94).

On the contrary, a chapel retrofitted for interfaith purposes could be a sign of increased religious diversity as religious minority congregations grow. The Muslim American Society center in Charlotte, NC is housed in what was a church. The pews, cross, and any Christian images were removed from the sanctuary to make room for a Musalla. In addition to the Musalla, the site houses a full-time Islamic school. Perhaps Muslims find retrofitting a building used for worship in another Abrahamic faith preferable to retrofitting a building formerly used for secular pursuits. An interfaith space could be created from an existing campus chapel if space and resources do not permit a separate prayer room.

Duke University is one institution that uses its chapel as a multifaith space. In addition to traditional Christian services, Duke chapel also hosts secular campus events and Jummah, the Muslim prayer service held on Fridays. Controversy erupted from Duke Chapel and Duke University's Muslim Student Association in January 2015 when the university announced that the *adhan*, the Muslim call to prayer, would be performed from the Duke Chapel bell tower. This announcement prompted a sharp criticism from evangelical Christian leaders (Jaschik, 2015). Opponents of the plan proclaimed that Duke, though religiously unaffiliated, was founded on Christian principles. The controversy and criticism could indicate a rift between Duke's current mission and its history. In the wake of terrorist attacks perpetrated by Muslim extremists, the Duke campus and surrounding community was particularly sensitive to attempts to promote religious pluralism.

Excerpts of Duke's mission statement can be interpreted to reference religious pluralism. However, the mission statement does not directly address religion.

> To these ends, the mission of Duke University is to ... promote a deep appreciation for the range of human difference.... By pursuing these

objectives with vision and integrity, Duke University seeks to engage the mind [and] elevate the spirit.

(Duke University, 2001)

Human differences can be interpreted to mean differences in religious and spiritual practices. Elevating can be interpreted to include spiritual interactions through religious worship.

Though the chapel is undeniably an important symbol to the entire Duke campus, it is still a Christian symbol. A chapel, by definition, is a place for Christian worship. No other religion uses the term "chapel" to identify a place of worship. The Duke campus is hospitable to Muslims and other religious minorities. In addition to an active Muslim Student Association, there are student organizations for Buddhists, Jews, Hindus and other religious minorities. Hosting Jummah in the basement of Duke Chapel is an example of interfaith cooperation and hospitality. However, the presence of hospitality does not eliminate bias. Eventually, the university announced that the *adhan* would be called from the lawn in front of the chapel. Perhaps the calling of the *adhan* from the bell tower made the lines between what is Christian and what is Islamic too ambiguous. Allen and Kellom (2001) describe the role of student affairs professionals when a campus crisis such as what happened at Duke makes headlines:

We are the ones called upon to interpret the mission of the institution in the midst of a campus crisis attracting media attention. In those times the real values of the college or university become clear. We are often asked to make sense of an institutional policy decision that has packed a student government meeting or made headlines in the student paper. We are the architects of the organizational culture in the residence halls, athletic departments, and student organizations. We may be the custodians of the collective soul of the campus.

(p. 55)

RELIGIOUS ATTIRE AND DRESS CODES

College campuses should provide safe spaces for students who wear religious attire. Religious attire can make students feel hyper-visible and draw unwanted attention from intolerant or prejudiced persons. College may also be a time when students experiment with religious attire or begin to wear it when they did not wear it previously. Hijab is one example. Though hijab is defined as any modest religious covering on a Muslim (man or woman), it is typically used to refer to the headscarves worn by Muslim women. Religious attire can have multiple meanings for those who wear it. Wearing religious

103

attire may help students become what they already are (Gurbuz & Gurbuz-Kucuksari, 2009). To explain the aforementioned statement, modern, secular society promotes the idea that a person has to find his or herself. For some students, wearing religious attire is a way to express their religious faith and grow more comfortable in their faith, thus becoming what they already are. Students who chose to wear religious attire such as hijab may be viewed by others as unmodernized, backward, closed minded, and/or radical (Gurbuz & Gurbuz-Kucuksari, 2009). Students who choose to wear religious attire may need extra support and accommodation.

Student dress codes are more common at private colleges. However, there are some public colleges that have implemented dress codes. Florida Agricultural & Mechanical University (FAMU) is one such institution. While Illinois State University does not have a campus-wide student dress code, this institution does allow units within the university to set dress codes. Moreover, the institution emphasizes that dress codes must impact all religious groups evenly (Illinois State University, 2014). This is an accommodation for religious minorities so that they are not unfairly burdened by a dress code. Colleges may implement dress codes for one of two reasons. The first reason is to maintain religious modesty and decorum in the campus environment. The dress code at Yeshiva University, an independent university under Jewish auspices, bans pants on women in academic buildings. Furthermore, skirts should be at least knee length and shirts must have sleeves. At Liberty University, a fundamentalist Christian institution in Virginia, dress codes are in place to uphold scriptural principals of modesty (Lipka, 2005). Liberty's dress code bans skirts above the knee on women and piercings on men, among other restrictions.

A second reason for campus dress codes is to encourage socially acceptable behavior in an educational or professional environment. Dress codes at HBCUs (Historically Black Colleges and Universities), such as FAMU, are usually implemented for the second reason, though religiously affiliated HBCUs may have dress codes for religious reasons as well. HBCU presidents believe that, when students dress down, academic performance and morale also goes down (Evans, 2008). FAMU and Hampton University, both HBCUs, use the exact same language to justify the implementation of a dress code:

The Dress Code [or Dress Standard] is based on the theory that learning to use socially acceptable manners and selecting attire appropriate to specific occasions and activities are critical factors in the total educational process. Understanding and employing these behaviors not only improves the quality of one's life, but also contributes to optimum morale, as well as embellishes the overall campus image. They also play a major role in instilling a sense of integrity and an appreciation for values and ethics.

(Florida A&M University, 2014; Hampton University, 2014)

Dress codes can indirectly restrict religious freedom. The dress code at both FAMU and Hampton University forbids indoor headgear. An exception is made for religious head coverings. However, Hampton students who wear religious head coverings and seek an exemption from the dress code headgear regulation must submit a request through Hampton's Office of the Chaplain (Murphy, 2013). While Hampton is private, it is not religiously affiliated. Yet, the approval of a Christian minister is required to wear religious head coverings representing any faith on campus. In this instance, interfaith support staff would be more appropriate for clearing exemptions to the headgear rule.

Another example of Christian privilege is the assumption that everyone is Christian. Clark (2003) defines Christian privilege as the unearned and unacknowledged advantages that Christians experience in their everyday lives. Clark goes on to provide examples of Christian privilege, such as the improper actions of one person not attributed to all people from a religious group and the mass media representing Christianity widely and positively.

Asking students to prove that they are of a certain faith just so they can wear their religious headgear on campus places an unfair and uncomfortable burden on the religious minority. As staff and administrators get to know students and encourage all students to learn about different religions, the difference between students who are wearing headgear for fashion and headgear out of religious obligation will be obvious. An argument for getting to know and understand students' religion and worldview before admonishing them about breaking the student dress code is demonstrated in the events at Hampton University.

RESIDENCE LIFE ISSUES AND OPTIONS

There are several issues related to residence life that can impact religious minorities. The first issue deals with resident assistants (RAs) and graduate assistants (GAs) working in residence halls. There is a fine line between rights of students and the responsibilities of RAs and GAs. For student employees, where do their rights as students end and their responsibilities as employees begin? Student workers such as RAs and GAs must be able to express their religious or spiritual beliefs without pressuring or coercing their subordinates or those under their responsibility. Even participating or organizing meetings as other students might, RAs must be cognizant of how they may be perceived by those of a different faith. Also, RAs must be approachable to all students regardless of differences in faith. Also, schools must be cognizant of the schedules of RA religious minorities who may not be able to work or attend staff meetings on certain days because of religious obligations or holy days. Making these sorts of accommodations might encourage religious diversity among residence hall staff.

The next issue is the availability of single-sex housing and co-educational visitation regulations. The availability of single-sex housing may present a challenge for some conservative religious minorities. Though students may have a non-religious preference for single-sex housing, for religiously conservative students a lack of single-sex housing may conflict with their religious values concerning opposite-sex interactions and thus be a deal breaker for living on campus.

Residence life on a college campus can be an opportunity for students to bond outside of the classroom. Residence life can also be a disaster if hall mates don't get along or feel that their needs are unmet. Interfaith houses and housing options are one way to bring awareness to religious minorities. However, colleges should see to it that all religious minorities are comfortable in whichever housing option the student chooses. Religion can be one of the ways schools match students for rooms and suites.

Students who are particularly devout may tend to live at home or in off-campus housing because they don't feel comfortable or there isn't enough support to build a religious life on campus. However, when students live at home, they don't get the benefits of living on campus. Research suggests that students who live on campus are more satisfied with their college experiences. Also living on campus provides more opportunities to interact with a diverse group. This is an opportunity for Christians and religious minorities to get to know one another outside of class.

By living on campus, students experience more physical diversity. Life in a residence hall places students in close contact with other students of different races, socio-economic statuses, abilities, and faiths. Residence halls and living/learning communities are opportunities for institutions to develop an awareness and appreciation for diversity. Commuter students are also in need of religious accommodations and opportunities to be engaged on campus. Research on African-American commuter students indicates that Greek life is an important conduit for the engagement of commuter students (Yearwood & Jones, 2012). Though the aforementioned study focused on African-American students, the results are relevant to religious minorities since the students in the study are minorities on the campus studied.

The mention of the uniquely American college Greek system may conjure images of wild and reckless parties. Greek life has relevance to, and the potential for positive impact on, religious minorities. Historically, membership in the mainstream Greek system was not an option for Jews and, in some cases, Catholics. According to Sanua (2010), if a student had just one-eighth of Jewish blood, this disqualified them from membership in a particular fraternity during the 1920s. Jewish fraternities and sororities were founded as a haven for Jewish students. The first Jewish fraternity, Pi Lambda Phi, was founded in 1895 at Yale University. These organizations continued to flourish throughout the first half of the 20th century. Particularly in small college towns where the benefit of a thriving Jewish community didn't exist, the Jewish Greek system provided a haven for Jewish students. Jewish Greek organizations served as a buffer from educational and housing discrimination experienced by Jewish college students (Sanua, 2010).

More recently, Muslim fraternities and sororities were founded to provide a Greek experience supported with Islamic principles to Muslim students. One of the first Muslim fraternities, Alpha Lambda Mu, was founded in 2013 at the University of Texas at Dallas (Spencer, 2014). The letters Alpha Lambda Mu were chose to represent Alif Lam Meem, the Arabic letter combinations that begin 29 suras of the Holy Qur'an. Alpha Upsilon Nu is another Muslim fraternity, incorporated in 2008. Gamma Gamma Chi is the first Muslim sorority. The sorority, founded in 2005, does not currently have collegiate chapters. Institutions should support the development of chapters of these organizations to appeal to religious minorities and increase their campus engagement through Greek life.

Practicing one's religion should be a simple execution on campus, whatever that religion is. Just like schools have other interest groups focused on subjects such as international studies or natural sciences, an interfaith housing area can be developed. An interfaith living and learning center would put religious minorities in closer contact with Christians who want to learn more about minority religions. Macalester College, a Presbyterian-affiliated college in Minnesota, has an interfaith house. Religious dietary restrictions are enforced in the kitchen of this house. Being around others who are different from oneself forces students to get to know themselves better and relate to others better. The residence hall provides the venue for this development. Students spend more hours in residence halls than in class. Also, interactions in the residence hall may be more intimate than classroom interactions.

CAMPUS EVENTS

Religious minorities may feel marginalized by traditions and practices. Formal campus activities may employ invocations or benedictions that connote Christianity. The prayer or benediction is often a Christian prayer. Institutions could invite clergy or dignitaries from other religions to offer a prayer during a ceremony. Also, a moment of reflection instead of a prayer may be appropriate.

Fried (2007) discusses the challenges of accommodating Muslim students as a director of residence life.

Ramadan occurs at different times in the year because of different calendars, and, over the course of my career, end of the year student affairs banquets occasionally occur during that holiday. When I was director of Residence Life, we had Moslem RAs on staff, and they were faced with an awkward dilemma – not attending the event and missing a very important opportunity to celebrate with their peers; attending and not eating; or violating their beliefs by attending and eating. At the very least, they were challenged to explain their behavior to their supervisors and to make choices that were, at the best, uncomfortable. At that point, these Moslem students were victims of the privileging of the Christian, non-Moslem calendar and related assumptions. A dialogue process helped to uncover a simple solution to this problem – holding the dinner after sundown, when observant Moslems may eat and celebrate. If the Moslem staff members worked in an institution where people were not familiar with their customs or expected all staff to conform without asking why some students were reluctant, the problem could not be addressed or solved.

(Fried, 2007, p. 5)

The culture at Fried's institution allowed for religious minorities to have their concerns addressed.

CALENDAR AND HOLIDAYS

Christian privilege is exemplified in an academic calendar that coincides with Christian practices (Clark, 2003). The inclusive campus recognizes the holy days of all religions, as well as Christian religions. Ali and Bagheri (2009) suggest including religious minority holidays on a calendar with a description of the holiday to help others learn about the event. Even if the holiday is not included on the academic calendar, an alternate calendar can be created. This is a way to show visible support for religious minorities. Acknowledgement is the key aspect with calendars and holidays. Religious minorities should see that their holidays are acknowledged, understood, and recognized even if the campus is not physically closed for that particular holiday. The calendar accommodation is an opportunity to acknowledge the faith of religious minorities and educate the campus community about religious holidays outside of Christian traditions. An action as simple as campus email blast about a religious minority holiday is an effort to make the campus environment more religiously inclusive. The College of Charleston, a public institution, has adopted a Statement of Religious Accommodation publicizing reasonable accommodations offered to students of all faiths and beliefs. The college's website also includes a list of religious minority holidays that may conflict with the university calendar and religious accommodation complaint form. The statement reads:

The College of Charleston community is enriched by students of many faiths that have various religious observances, practices and beliefs. We value student rights and freedoms, including the right of each student to adhere to individual systems of religion. The College prohibits discrimination against any student because of such student's religious belief or any absence thereof. The College acknowledges that religious practices differ from tradition to tradition and that the demands of religious observance in some traditions may cause conflicts with student schedules. In affirming this diversity, like many other colleges and universities, the College supports the concept of "reasonable accommodation for religious observance" in regard to class attendance, and the scheduling of examinations and other academic work requirements, unless the accommodation would create an undue hardship on the College. Faculty are required, as part of their responsibility to students and the College, to ascribe to this policy and to ensure its fair and full implementation. The accommodation request imposes responsibilities and obligations on both the individual requesting the accommodation and the College. Faculty members are expected to reasonably accommodate individual religious practices. Examples of reasonable accommodations for student absences might include: rescheduling of an exam or giving a make-up exam for the student in question; altering the time of a student's presentation; allowing extra-credit assignments to substitute for missed class work or arranging for an increased flexibility in assignment dates. Regardless of any accommodation that may be granted, students are responsible for satisfying all academic objectives, requirements and prerequisites as defined by the instructor and by the College.

(College of Charleston, 2014)

ATHLETICS

Athletics presents an additional challenge to accommodating religious minorities. Game and practice schedules can conflict with religious practices and holidays. During the holy month of Ramadan, Muslims abstain from eating and drinking during daylight hours. Abstaining from food and water can make athletic practices and games an extreme challenge for Muslim athletes. Also, Ramadan moves back 10 days on the Christian/solar calendar each year. Therefore, Ramadan does not fall at the exact same day or date each year.

Coaches and athletic directors can accommodate Muslim athletes and other students who may participate in religious fasts by adjusting workouts so they are less strenuous during the warmest hours. Some Muslim athletes opt not to fast and to make up the days. Muslims are not the only students who may participate in a religious fast. Student athletes participating in a religious fast should not feel pressure to break their fasts and understand that the decision to fast or not to fast is theirs alone.

College football is often referred to as a religion in the South. Babb (2014) explains:

> In this part of America, college football fits somewhere between pastime and obsession, and like church, it is more than a weekend activity. Nothing says more about a Southerner than the team he cheers on Saturdays and the church he attends on Sundays.
>
> (p. 1)

Comparing college football to religion is appropriate for a discussion of religious inclusiveness within college sports. In an effort to build team unity, football players often participate in extracurricular activities off the field. On some campuses, participation in football takes an overly Christian tone. The Fellowship of Christian Athletes, an interdenominational organization, is one organization in which college athletes participate. Athletes in Action, an athletics auxiliary of the evangelical Christian organization Campus Crusade for Christ, is another organization where student athletes can combine their passion for sports and Christianity. Football coaches at some institutions encourage players to attend church services together, coordinating trips and even providing school-sponsored transportation.

Clemson University is one institution criticized for encouraging church attendance. DeAndre Hopkins, who currently plays for the Houston Texans, was baptized as a student and football player at Clemson. The baptism took place at a football field on Clemson's campus. Since 1999, Clemson's football program has sponsored a Church Day where players attend a church service together with the coach. Coaches at Clemson even go so far as to mention Christianity during the recruiting process as an assurance that future student athletes will receive spiritual guidance as well as academic and athletic guidance. The University of Mississippi (Ole Miss) is another college where football players are encouraged to worship as Christians. Church services are held inside the football practice facility. Both Clemson and Ole Miss are public institutions. Football coaching staffers are trying to meet the spiritual needs of its student athletes. College athletes, particularly at Division I institutions like Clemson and Ole Miss, are under tremendous pressure to perform on and off the field. DeBerg (2002) explains:

> There are several major dynamics at work that marry evangelical Christianity to college athletics, even at state supported and non-sectarian colleges and universities. First, there is enormous pressure on coaches to field

winning teams. If religious activities, advisors, worship and prayer seem to boost player morale and confidence, and if religion increases team cohesiveness and unity then coaches, untrained in the First Amendment and in the varieties of American religion, are likely to welcome the attention and activities of campus ministers, especially those that claim special concern for student athletes and special expertise in ministering to them. And the coaches themselves are more and more likely, with the growth of campus athletics ministries to have experience in these ministries and to be formed into this kind of religious culture.

(p. 2)

Every college football player wants to maintain a good relationship with their coach. If coaches are encouraging and sponsoring church attendance, players may attend church services to remain in good favor with their coach. There is a fine line between encouraging personal development through religion and unduly influencing college football players to attend church services. DeBerg (2002) underscores the potential for religious coercion:

Is it possible, really, for players to resist their coaches when it comes to attending team "chapel," for example? Or to refuse to recite the Lord's Prayer when the head coach asks the team to do so before and after every game?

(p. 3)

The opportunity to nourish one's spirituality is useful in the least. However, these efforts may be too biased toward Christianity. Perhaps the efforts to develop the spiritual lives of student athletes should be interreligious, allowing those questioning their religious foundation or believing different from Christianity to explore in an environment that acknowledges religious pluralism. College athletics doesn't have to be secular, just more inclusive.

As mentioned previously in this chapter, U.S. courts have determined that the offering of a prayer during campus events at public colleges does not amount to the establishment of religion. However, DeBerg (2002) believes activities beyond a simple prayer offering may amount to religious establishment if there were a legal challenge. She draws concern to practices such as prayer meetings and church services held in athletic facilities under the auspices of athletics programs and questions whether or not these practices would pass the "establishment of religion" test posed by the First Amendment. Given the increasing popularity of evangelical Christian organizations for college athletes, institutions should be aware of the potential for religious coercion in the athletic setting.

111

ADDITIONAL ACCOMMODATIONS

Another way to accommodate religious minorities is to encourage students to study abroad in places like Israel, Saudi Arabia, or India. Encourage religious minority students to explore their identities by participating in educational trips to regions of significance to religious minorities. Also, campus libraries can accommodate religious minorities by maintaining a collection of materials on world religions as well as items on Atheism and Agnosticism.

CONCLUSION

This chapter has addressed how institutions can accommodate religious minority students. Before appropriate accommodations can be enacted, administrators must understand what religious minorities need to comfortably practice their faith on campus. Specifically discussed were the availability of interfaith prayer/meditation rooms, religiously compliant dining options, such as kosher, halal, and/or selections, headgear regulations, and chaplain services. Consideration of holidays outside of the mainline Protestant tradition when creating the academic calendar and housing options for religious minorities and other related campus accommodations were also discussed in this chapter. All campuses have an obligation to meet the needs of their religious minority students. The whole student will not be educated if his or her spiritual life is neglected. All students should feel comfortable in practicing their religion and sharing their religious beliefs on campus.

Scholars have long referred to higher education as a business (Christensen & Eyring, 2011; Altbach, Gumport, & Berdahl, 2011). Businesses need clients or customers to thrive and remain financially stable. Students are the customers in the higher education industry. Every institution of higher learning is interested in maintaining a strong enrollment. Therefore, institutions of higher learning cannot afford to recruit only Christian students. If colleges can recruit students from diverse religious backgrounds, they must also accommodate these students when they arrive on campus, supporting their persistence and growth.

To accommodate religious minority students, institutions must be exemplary hosts. In an interview with Libby Nelson, Douglas and Rhonda Hustedt Jacobsen (co-directors of the Religion in the Academy project at Messiah College) elaborate on how colleges serve as good hosts from the perspective of religious diversity.

Being a good host means first of all understanding who one is hosting. In the case of religion, this means recognizing the very real diversity of religion that exists on any given campus. Hosting also involves being respectful of one's guests – i.e., students. In relation to religion, this means looking for positive points of connection between personal religious perspectives and the learning experience. Obviously higher education has a responsibility to be critical of religion as well as respectful of it, but respect is a necessary counterpoint to criticism. Finally, a good host also encourages conversations and nourishes interpersonal relationships, which in the area of religion means encouraging constructive interfaith conversation and friendship, not only among different religions, but also across the lines of difference represented by religious views of the world and other secular faiths or moral life stances.

(Nelson, 2012)

DISCUSSION QUESTIONS

1. Before selecting a college or university to attend, what considerations should religious minority students be concerned with?
2. What are the most desirable campus accommodations that religious minority students may be interested in?
3. How might universities be proactive in meeting the needs of religious minority students as opposed to reactive?
4. Is it unfair for public universities funded by tax payer dollars to concern themselves with accommodating religious minorities?
5. Would you assert that it is more cost effective on the part of the university to have religious accommodations that cater to many religious minority groups on campus or just a few. Please explain your answer.

REFERENCES

Ali, S.R., & Bagheri, E. (2009). Practical suggestions to accommodate the needs of Muslim students on campus. *New Directions for Student Services, 125,* 47–54.

Allen, K.E., & Kellom, G.E. (2001). The role of spirituality in student affairs and staff development. *New Directions for Student Services, 95,* 47–55.

Altbach, P.G., Gumport, P.J., & Berdahl, R.O. (2011). *American Higher Education in the 21st Century: Social, Political, and Economic Challenges.* Baltimore, MD: Johns Hopkins University Press.

Babb, K. (2014, August 29). Where college football is religion and religion shapes college football. *Washington Post.* Retrieved from www.washingtonpost.com/sports/colleges/where-college-football-is-a-religion-and-religion-shapes-college-football/2014/08/29/8d03de32-2dfa-11e4-bb9b-997ae96fad33_story.html.

Blumenfeld, W.J., & Klein, J.R. (2009). Working with Jewish undergraduates. *New Directions for Student Services, 125,* 33–38.

Bowman, N.A., & Small, J.L. (2013). The experiences and spiritual growth of religiously privileged and religiously marginalized college students. In A. Bryant Rockenbach & M. Mayhew (eds) *Spirituality in College Students' Lives*. New York, NY: Routledge.

Chaudhuri v. *Tennessee*, 130 F.3d 232 (6th Cir. 1997).

Christensen, C.M., & Eyring, H.J. (2011). *The Innovative University: Changing the DNA of Higher Education from the Inside Out*. San Francisco, CA: Jossey-Bass.

Clark, C. (2003). Diversity initiatives in higher education: A case study of multicultural organizational development through the lens of religion, spirituality, faith and secular inclusion. *Multicultural Education, 10*, 52–57.

College of Charleston. (2014). *Statement on Religious Accommodation*. Retrieved from http://president.cofc.edu/community-relations/rlc/accommodation.php.

Dallavis, C. (2011). "Because that's who I am": Extending theories of culturally responsible pedagogy to consider religious identity, belief, and practice. *Multicultural Perspectives, 13*(3), 138–144.

DeBerg, B.A. (2002). Athletes and religion on campus. *Peer Review, 4*(4), 10.

Duke University. (2001). *Mission Statement*. Retrieved from http://trustees.duke.edu/governing/mission.php.

Engel v. *Vitale*, 370 U.S. 421 1962.

Evans, J. (2008). The Dress CODE. *Black Collegian, 39*(1), 16–20.

Florida Agricultural & Mechanical University. (2014). *Dress Standards*. Retrieved from www.famu.edu/index.cfm?dressstandard&DressStandards.

Fried, J. (2007, Summer). Religious privilege: Dialogue or domination? In *Developments, 5*(2). Retrieved from www.myacpa.org/publications/developments/volume-5-issue-2.

Geiger, R. (2011). Ten generations of higher education. In P.G. Altbach, R.O. Berdahl, & P.J. Gumport (eds) *American Higher Education in the 21st Century*. Baltimore, MD: Johns Hopkins University Press.

Gilliat-Ray, S. (2000). *Religion in Higher Education: The Politics of the Multi-Faith Campus*. Surrey, England: Ashgate.

Gurbuz, M., & Gurbuz-Kucuksari, G. (2009). Between sacred codes and secular consumer society: The practice of headscarf adoption among American college girls. *Journal of Muslim Minority Affairs 29*(3), 387–399.

Hampton University. (2014). *Dress Code*. Retrieved from www.hamptonu.edu/student_life/dresscode.cfm.

Illinois State University. (2014). *University Policy and Procedures*. Retrieved from http://policy.illinoisstate.edu/academic/4-1-4.shtml.

Jaschik, S. (2015, January 16). Praying for respect. *Inside Higher Ed*. Retrieved from www.insidehighered.com/news/2015/01/16/duke-facing-opposition-evangelists-drops-plan-allow-muslim-call-prayer-chapel-tower.

Kadushin, C., & Tighe, E. (2008). How hard is it to be a Jew on college campuses? *Contemporary Jewry, 28,* 38–57.

Kaplin, W.A., & Lee, B.A. (2007). *The Law of Higher Education* San Francisco, CA: Jossey-Bass.

Kazanjian, V., Keen, J., & Laurence, P. (2010). Building a new global commons: Religious diversity and the challenge for higher education. *Journal of Interreligious Dialogue, 4,* 29–37.

Kocet, M., & Stewart, D. (2011). The role of student affairs in promoting religious and secular pluralism and interfaith cooperation. *Journal of College & Character, 12*(1) (Online). doi: 10.2202/1940-1639.1762.

Kuh, G.D., & Gonyea, R.M. (2006). Spirituality, liberal learning and college student engagement. *Liberal Education, 92*(1), 40–47.

Lee v. *Weisman,* 505 U.S 577 (1992).

Lipka, S. (2005). Liberty U. updates its dress code: Shorts are OK; "Daisy Dukes" are not. *Chronicle Of Higher Education, 52*(2), A47.

McIntosh, P. (1989, July/August). White privilege: Unpacking the invisible knapsack. *Peace and Freedom.* Retrieved from www.areteadventures.com/articles/white_privilege_unpacking_the_invisible_napsack.pdf.

Moran, C.D., Roberts, C.J., Tobin, J.A., & Harvey, L.M. (2008). Religious expression among residents and resident assistants in residence halls at public colleges and universities: Freedoms and constraints. *Journal of College & University Student Housing, 35*(2), 48–61.

Murphy, R. (2013, October 8). Reports: Hampton student forced to get approval to wear religious headgear. *The Daily Press.* Retrieved from http://articles.dailypress.com/2013-10-08/news/dp-nws-hampton-hajab-papers-20131008_1_yuri-milligan-hampton-student-headscarf.

Nelson, L. (2012, October 25) No longer invisible. *Inside Higher Ed*. Retrieved from www.insidehighered.com/news/2012/10/25/book-argues-colleges-should-do-better-job-engaging-religion.

Rosenberger v. *Rector and Visitors of the University of Virginia,* 515 U.S. 819 (1995).

Sanua, M.R. (2000). Jewish college fraternities in the United States, 1895–1968: An overview. *Journal Of American Ethnic History, 19*(2), 3.

Schlosser, L.Z. (2003). Christian privilege: Breaking a sacred taboo. *Journal of Multicultural Counseling and Development, 31,* 44–51.

Seifert, T. (2007). Understanding Christian privilege: Managing the tensions of spiritual plurality. *About Campus, 12*(2), 10–17.

Sorrentino, P.V. (2010). What do college students want? A student centered approach to multifaith involvement. *Journal of Ecumenical Studies, 45*(1), 79–96.

Spencer, K. (2014, February 6). Fraternity life, Islamic style. *New York Times.* Retrieved from www.nytimes.com/2014/02/09/education/edlife/greek-life-islamic-style.html.

Tanford v. *Brand,* 104 F.3d 982 (7th Cir. 1997).

Widmar v. *Vincent,* 454 U.S. 263 (1981).

Yearwood, T.L., & Jones, E.A. (2012). Understanding what influences successful black commuter students' engagement in college. *JGE: The Journal Of General Education, 61*(2), 97–125.

Chapter 6

Conclusion

Chapter 1 provided an overview of religious diversity in the United States and on college campuses. Empirical research on religious minority college students was covered in Chapter 2. Chapter 3 discussed campus assessment and how institutions can assess their campus culture and implement strategic plans to reach religious diversity goals. Religious diversity in the college classroom was discussed in Chapter 4. Campus accommodations for religious minority students was the subject of Chapter 5. This chapter will provide student affairs practitioners and administrators with recommendations for practice and discuss the intersection of race and religion.

Colleges face a sociological imperative to respond to religious minority students. There are two issues discouraging dialogue on religious diversity in higher education. The first issue is a bias or cultural propensity toward Christianity. This book is not meant to be an attack on Christianity or mainline Protestants. Rather, it is a humble confrontation of homogeny in religious and spiritual life on college campuses. The second issue is the secularization of higher education.

Though the first American institutions of higher learning were church affiliated, secularism has dominated American higher education in recent decades. Kazanjian et al. (2010) explain how the shift toward secularism occurred:

Although it was religiously-inspired motivation that led to the founding of many of the earliest colleges and universities in this country and shaped early educational philosophy and pedagogy, it is the assumption of a single, shared religious context and a common religious language to describe the educational ideals of higher education that forged a too small container in the years that followed. The restrictions placed on belief and thought in colleges and universities by religious institutions led to the growing objections of many scholars who found their intellectual inquiry restricted by the theological principals rather than educational ones.

> Gradually, secular scholarship won out: most colleges and universities severed ties with organized religion and replaced religious frameworks with secular ones for life on campus.
>
> (p. 30)

As state universities and land-grant institutions entered the higher education landscape, secularism increased. The shift from an overwhelmingly private higher education system to an overwhelming public one abandoned the Christian roots of higher education. Despite this abandonment, the "too small container" Kazanjian speaks of has encapsulated nuances of Christianity while pressing attention to religion, spirituality, and religious minorities to the margins of student affairs. Secular trends are even impacting religiously affiliated institutions. According to Woodrow (2004), religiously affiliated institutions have removed religious words from their names. The market of higher education makes these changes necessary in order to appeal to a broader range of students. Finances transform formerly Christian-affiliated colleges to independent colleges with Christian backgrounds as financial resources from religious denominations decline.

> Our university and college campuses focus a great deal of attention on diversity. This is a proper focus for higher education and one that is needed in our society. Religious diversity, however, is often left off the agenda and may be subsumed under a rising tide of secular animosity that says there is no place for religious expression in the academy.
>
> (Sorrentino, 2010, p. 79)

This quote summarizes the idea that higher education should be a secular space, particularly outside of religiously affiliated institutions. Hollinger (2002) discusses the perception that higher education has gone secular, separating from its religious roots. "Our leading colleges and universities once shared in a pervasive Protestant culture, to which they owe a great deal. Now, however, mainstream academia maintains a certain critical distance from the Christian project" (Hollinger, 2002, p. 40). Higher education should become less secular by embracing all religions and spiritual traditions. Colleges can promote the religious and spiritual leanings of students without indoctrinating or proselytizing. How do colleges become less secular but less Christian? The authors acknowledge that desiring a less secular and less Christian higher education is a paradox. The goal is to embrace faith, spirituality, and worldviews beyond Christianity.

IDENTITY DEVELOPMENT

Identity helps students understand who they are. Religious identity is a constantly evolving process. College may be the first time students begin to ponder and develop their religious identity. College students should have the opportunity to develop a strong religious identity, whatever their identification is: Christian, Jewish, Muslim, Hindu, other religious minority, Atheist, Agnostic, or other worldview. How does religious identity develop in college students and how can colleges facilitate this development? Religious minority students want to maintain their identity while engaging with the broader campus community. The potential conflict between religious identity and the campus community is one that religious majority students do not have to consider.

Affirming identity is one third of Tatum's (2000) ABC approach to creating climates of engagement on diverse campuses. The acronym ABC stands for affirming identity, building community, and cultivating leadership. Religious minorities must have their identity affirmed by seeing reflections of themselves on their campuses. This reflection can be viewed through a myriad of ways: in faculty and staff, in other students, as well as in programming. The creation of an interfaith spiritual center is one way to affirm the identity of religious minorities while affirming a place for Christians on a religiously diverse campus. All students must have their identity affirmed before leadership can be cultivated within a diverse community.

Fisherman (2002) identified three types of religious identity development: healthy, unhealthy, and dangerous. Healthy identity development involves intrinsically motivated faith. Students with healthy religious identity development are able to reconcile their behavior and their beliefs. With unhealthy religious identity development, there is discouragement from religious exploration. Students may get entangled into what Fisherman identifies as four categories: slogans, diffuse spiritual identity, moratorium, and foreclosure. Students with unhealthy religious identity development may cling to slogans as a response to religious questions to which they have not processed answers. Students with a diffuse spiritual identity avoid reconciling their identity and discussing his or her religious beliefs for fear of having to resolve them. A moratorium, or delay in development, can lead to a positive or negative religious identity development. Students will either make a personal decision regarding religious issues or experiment beyond their moral boundaries. When unhealthy religious development forecloses, religious rituals are promoted in order to join a certain group. Students whose religious identity is developing dangerously may join a cult where critical thinking is discouraged or become obsessed with a charismatic religious leader. Alienation and inconsistency may also manifest among students with dangerous religious identity development. Students may become alienated and avoid religion. Inconsistent students may participate in certain religious practices depending on the context and occasion.

The concept of doubt is important in religious identity development. Doubt encourages students to learn more about their own beliefs and others' beliefs: "…doubt is a part of the process of exploration and crisis and therefore an important element in attaining identity achievement" (Baltazar & Coffen, 2011). Students will either confirm their preconceived notions about religion or change their minds and decide to further explore a different path. Doubt through the process of identity development is the type of growth and self-knowledge that colleges and universities are charged with facilitating.

Religious doubt can also manifest through spiritual struggle. Bryant and Astin (2008) define doubt as: "an experience familiar to many students whose college years are marked by reflections on faith, purpose, and life meaning and by efforts to understand the preponderance of suffering, evil, and death in the world" (p. 1). Which college students' characteristics are associated with spiritual struggle? Research conducted by Bryant and Astin concludes that being a religious minority, female, enrolled at religiously affiliated colleges, a psychology major, or exposed to unfamiliar worldviews are all associated with spiritual struggle during the college years (2008, p. 20). In particular, women of religious minorities are more likely to struggle spiritually. Student affairs practitioners should work to impede spiritual struggle because spiritual struggle can negatively impact students' self-esteem and physical health. Bryant and Astin express why spiritual struggle is worth the attention of college personnel.

> The spiritual realm and the deeper life questions it brings to light do play a role in the young adult journey, making the attention to these issues on the part of practitioners, administrators, and faculty a clear necessity. Indeed there are critical implications of struggling spiritually that are intimately tied to students' sense of well-being and adjustment to the adult world. Failure to recognize the seriousness of these facets of students' lives is to leave them quite alone on their quest to understand central issues of meaning. Thus, the initial step for higher education is take note of and seek to appreciate the varieties of spiritual struggling and their significance.
>
> (Bryant & Astin, 2008, p. 23)

Struggle does not have to have negative outcomes for students. Students can emerge from spiritual struggle more certain of their beliefs and more knowledgeable of others' beliefs.

SEPARATION OF CHURCH AND STATE

Separation of church and state is the phrase used to describe the absence of an official church or religion in the United States. Public colleges and universities can use the separation of church and state argument to defend a secular campus. However, the phrase "church and state" itself is biased because it assumes that everyone attends a church if they attend any venue of worship at all. A better term would be separation of religion and state. Schlosser (2003) explains the bias in the phrase separation of church and state: "Inherent in a discussion of church and state is the ethnocentric assumption that either (a) church means the same thing for everybody or (b) church means something for everybody" (p. 46).

Institutions of higher learning are slowly but surely embracing religious pluralism. Sorrentino (2010) argues that there are at least four definitions of religious pluralism. The first definition is, arguably, the most common: civility and tolerance in regards to all religions. A second meaning of religious pluralism is inclusive particularity, which affirms religious differences while highlighting commonalities. The third meaning of religious pluralism is probably the most controversial. Exclusive commonality, where differences are ignored in order to focus on what unifies various religions. Differences are what make each religion unique. Exclusive commonality is more likely than inclusive particularity to become a focus on what other religions have in common with Christianity instead of what each religion has in common with the other. Campuses must stride a precarious walk between inclusive particularity and exclusive particularity, embracing differences and commonalities between different religions and worldviews. Below is a checklist that institutions can use to briefly assess engagement with religion.

RELIGIOUS DIVERSITY CHECKLIST

- Religion is mentioned in reference to diversity.
- Strategic plan includes objectives related to religious diversity.
- There are accountability mechanisms for religious diversity on campus.
- Religious organizations in the local community are linked to religious diversity efforts on campus.
- There are short- and long-term goals for religious inclusion and the campus community is informed of these goals.
- Resources are allocated toward religious diversity efforts.
- Campus committees are comprised of religiously diverse members.

ENGAGING AROUND RELIGION

Why is it so difficult to discuss religion? What makes practitioners reluctant to approach religion? One myth about encouraging students to embrace their own religion is that students will get so involved in their own religion that they have difficulty learning about other religions. This myth is disproven by organizations like the Interfaith Youth Core. A non-profit that works with college students to promote interfaith cooperation, the Chicago-based Interfaith Youth Core (IFYC), was founded in 2002. IFYC uses campus partnerships and leadership institutes to achieve its mission. College students representing all religions and worldviews participate in IFYC's programs. Difficult dialogue must take place before student affairs practitioners can develop a religiously inclusive campus environment. Student affairs practitioners work to enrich the whole student. Religion and spirituality or belief traditions are a part of every student's identity in some form. Watt (2007) defines difficult dialogue as the verbal or written exchange of ideas or opinions among citizens within a community that centers on an awakening of potentially conflicting views about beliefs and values. Watt (2007) goes on to explain in detail what makes dialogue around religious privilege difficult. Figure 6.1 shows the three elements of difficult dialogue.

Student affairs practitioners are incompetent in the area of religious diversity unless they understand their own values, beliefs, and perspectives on religion. Self-awareness is key before these professionals can effectively engage around religious diversity. Student affairs practitioners must attend to their

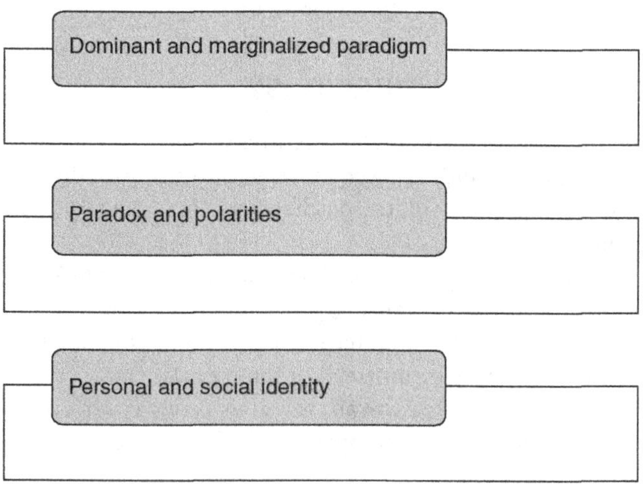

Figure 6.1 Watt's (2007) Three Elements of Difficult Dialogue

own spiritual needs before they can address the spiritual needs of students. Allen and Kellom (2001) explain:

> We are managers and supervisors who have arrived at a position of influence with responsibility for training and retaining our personnel. The precious budget dollars in the professional development line items are a critical way in which we can offer meaningful staff meetings and workshops to boost productivity. Those goals cannot be accomplished without consideration of the whole person when working with the staff. There is no more central part of the whole person than the spirit.
>
> (p. 47)

Though Allen and Kellom differentiate between spirituality and religion, the authors argue that one cannot address their spirituality without acknowledging their religious beliefs as one way of expressing their spirituality. Though the terms *religion* and *spirituality* have different meanings, they are often used interchangeably. One term is rarely discussed without the other. The frenetic, outcomes-based nature of college student affairs work can impede professionals from actualizing their spiritual lives.

Student affairs workers must first educate themselves about various religions, faith traditions, and belief systems. The trainer must be trained. This training includes education about the history of religious minorities in the United States. For campus educators to work effectively with religious minorities on college campuses, they must have an understanding of the issues contributing to religious minority identity development.

Also, student affairs professionals should not expect religious minority students to teach the religious majority about their faith. Religious minority students may feel hyper-visible or imposed upon if it is automatically expected that they will share about their beliefs. These students may also fear the reaction to different perspectives and rituals, or fear that they will be expected to possess scholarly knowledge on a minority religion, or that they will be viewed as a token representative for an entire faith. Students may share about their religious beliefs but the burden is on professionals to learn. Understanding minority religions means more than learning rote facts, celebrating holidays, or eating traditional foods. Interfaith programming will not progress without understanding the experiences of all religions and traditions. Student affairs practitioners should develop relationships with local clergy and religious leaders, especially if religious leaders are not employed or volunteering to serve the campus.

Student affairs practitioners help students shape their *faith frame*. According to Small (2009), the faith frame is the lens through which students see the world. "These faith frames are linked to students' awareness of religious marginalization in society" (Small, 2009, p. 13). Student affairs practitioners can normalize the religious minority perspective by openly talking about religious minorities and providing information about various religions and belief traditions to the campus community. Religious diversity is the responsibility of all student affairs professionals, not just those assigned to multicultural affairs or similar units. In some student affairs preparation programs, diversity is taught as a subject of study instead of a culture to actualize. Student affairs practitioners must not only understand diversity but be prepared to execute diverse principles in their work. Also, student affairs practitioners can challenge the ways of thinking about spirituality by acknowledging all belief or non-belief perspectives in all campus programming related to religion and spirituality. Student affairs staff should review their institutional mission, history, and strategic plans for relevance to interfaith cooperation and religious pluralism. By adding religious diversity onto existing diversity programs, student affairs administrators can reduce the likelihood of resistance from the campus community. The focus of the student affairs practitioner should be on providing students with opportunities for interfaith engagement in order to alleviate religious tension and improve the campus religious climate.

The following steps outline the skills student affairs practitioners need to develop to effectively handle interfaith issues. The steps are adapted from Sue et al.'s (1982) Multicultural Competence Model. The first step is to develop interfaith awareness: attitudes, values, beliefs, self-awareness, and the assumptions needed to serve students who are religiously different from oneself. The second step is to increase interfaith knowledge: preconceptions about others' religions, values, and beliefs. Inaccurate information needs to be corrected before student affairs professionals can achieve interfaith competence. The third step is the development of interfaith skills: meaningful interactions that allow student affairs practitioners to understand religious differences. Once interfaith skills are developed, student affairs practitioners can work toward improving religiously diverse environments.

Religious diversity work must include perspectives outside of traditional faith traditions and deities. The term *religious minority* is actually a misnomer because it assumes that everyone adheres to a religion. Perhaps the term *belief minority* is a better descriptor for students who don't adhere to any religion, such as Atheists. Seventeen percent of college students report adhering to no religion (Goodman & Mueller, 2009). That is a sizeable minority. This book may not adequately address Atheist and Agnostic students since most of the discussion here surrounds religion and faith. Whether you believe in one God, no God, or many Gods, you are a belief minority if you are not Christian.

Understanding minority religions will not automatically create an inclusive campus climate. Creating a religiously inclusive campus climate takes more than data, more than just learning about different religions. Creating a religiously inclusive campus culture takes more than designated weeks highlighting the food, dress, traditions, and rituals of different religions. Student affairs practitioners should take advantage of student tendencies to explore different views and question their own values while promoting interfaith cooperation among students. Interfaith harmony won't happen after a weekend campus retreat. The process of accommodating religious minorities and reflecting on interfaith conflicts is ongoing. The development of interfaith awareness, knowledge, and skills is also ongoing.

Student affairs practitioners, as well as students, should not only have a seat at the religious diversity table but also have a slice of PIE (Privileged Identity Exploration). Watt's (2007) Privileged Identity Exploration (PIE) model is one method student affairs practitioners can use to encourage students to explore religious privilege. The PIE method encourages meaningful discussions by identifying eight defensive reactions to reflecting on one's social, political, and economic position in society. The model also provides student affairs workers with examples of the types of resistance they might receive from students while exploring religious privilege. Watt gives potential responses to defenses from religious majority members. The six assumptions of Watt's PIE model are:

1. The exploration of religiously privileged identity is an ongoing socialization process.
2. There is no ultimate level of consciousness that can be reached regarding one's religiously privileged identity.
3. Engaging in difficult dialogue is a necessary part of unlearning religious oppression.
4. Defense modes are normal human reactions to the uncertainty that one feels when exploring their religiously privileged identities thoroughly.
5. Defense modes are expressed in identifiable behaviors.
6. Expressions of defense modes may vary by situation.

There are three categories of responses in Watt's PIE model, as seen in Figure 6.2. The eight types of responses are categorized as either recognizing, contemplating, or addressing privileged religious identity.

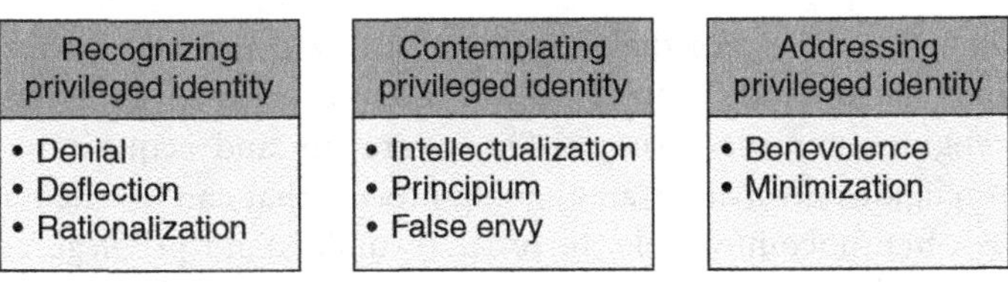

Figure 6.2 Three Types of Responses in Watt's (2007) PIE Model

The following is a brief description and example of the eight types of responses in Watt's PIE model.

1. A *denial* response is exemplified by arguing that religious bias doesn't exist. "Everyone is free to practice whatever religion they want. The local Target even has Hanukkah decorations."

2. A *deflection* response focuses on a person's background or education as a reason to avoid the realities of religious bias and discrimination. "There weren't many __________ (Jews, Muslims, Hindus, etc.) where I grew up, so I was rarely exposed to people who were not Christian."

3. A *rationalization* response uses logic to explain religious bias. "Most of the students on this campus are Christian, so it makes sense that we put up Christmas decorations and close on Good Friday."

4. An *intellectualization* response focuses on facts or events to avoid discussing religious bias. "I understand that Muslims might be unfairly profiled. However, with all of the terrorist attacks perpetrated by Muslims, it makes sense to be suspicious of them."

5. A *principium* defense is exemplified by avoiding exploration of other religions based on one's own religious beliefs. "My beliefs are firmly rooted in Christianity. I'm not interested in converting to another religion. Therefore, I'm not really interested in learning about another religion."

6. A *false envy* response is exemplified by admiring or exoticizing a characteristic of religious minorities. "I wish I wore a hijab. It would make bad hair days so much easier."

7. A *benevolence* response focuses on charitable acts as a substitute for confronting religious bias. "My club is fundraising to send supplies to Syria. I understand the importance of helping the less fortunate, regardless of their faith."

8. A *minimization* response focuses on rote facts about religious minorities instead of religious bias and privilege. "I would like to learn about other religions, what their adherents believe, and their rituals. If I learn these facts, I will be better prepared to interact with them."

Watt (2007, p. 15) argues that a multiculturally competent student affairs professional understands that he or she will never learn everything about various religious minority groups. The awareness and acquisition of skills related to religious diversity is an ongoing process that can be uncomfortable. Growth is often uncomfortable. In order to understand privilege and social oppression, students must make a connection between intellect and emotions (Young & Davis-Russell, 2003). When the intellect and emotions collide over religious diversity, the result is an uncomfortable but necessary state of mind that will lead to greater understanding of religious minorities. Figure 6.3 displays an equation for diverse dialogue leading to a greater understanding of religious diversity.

The following framework is an additional method for student exploration of religious privilege and religious diversity. This framework is adapted from Ortiz and Rhoads' (2000) Multicultural Education Framework.

1. Understanding religion: Students understand their own religion and/or beliefs, explore who they are, and learn how to socially interact with a religiously diverse population. Students understand how religion shapes aspects of their daily lives.

2. Learning about other cultures: Students learn about different religions and develop an understanding of others' religious values, behaviors, and traditions.

3. Recognizing and deconstructing Christian privilege: Students learn that Christianity is the norm that determines acceptable behaviors, cultures, and traditions. Deconstructing Christian privilege requires skilled facilitation of dialogue in order for students to understand how Christian privilege affects students' lives. The step may be uncomfortable for Christian students since it aims to teach them how to confront their own privilege.

4. Recognizing multiple religions: Students engage in recognizing the legitimacy of diverse religions. The goal of this step is to promote religious pluralism.

5. Developing an interfaith outlook: Students learn about the complex interconnections between religion, society, and individuals. Students understand that diverse religions comprise democratic societies where people of all faiths are represented.

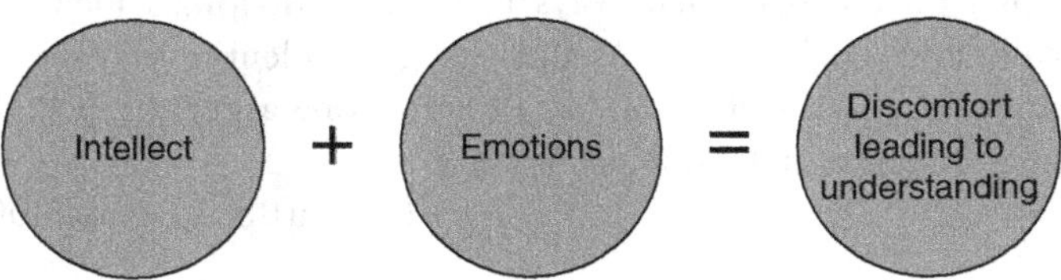

Figure 6.3 Equation for Diverse Dialogue Leading to a Greater Understanding of Religious Diversity

RACE AND RELIGION

Issues of race and religion are often intertwined, with groups facing discrimination and bias because of their faith or color. However, religious diversity does not have the strong implications on academic success often associated with racial diversity. One difference between racial privilege and religious privilege is that, while Christians will claim and acknowledge their faith as Christians, Whites typically do not acknowledge race or their Whiteness in the same fashion. "Various types of oppression often interact, producing additive effects; being a member of multiple minority groups increases the likelihood and frequency of experiencing oppression and discrimination" (Schlosser, 2003, p. 45).

The great sociologist W.E.B. DuBois declared the color line the problem of the 20th century. Race is also, arguably, the problem of the 21st century. In many ways, religious minorities can be placed in a dichotomy similar to a White/non-White dichotomy. According to Fried (2007), the North American culture encourages our tendency to think in either/or times. Everything is not Black or White, pun intended. Even throughout this book, students are discussed in terms of Christian and non-Christian even though non-Christians may be as different from each other as they are from Christians.

Students balance multiple identities, of which race and religion are just two. For students of color who also happen to not be Christian, their marginalization is multiplied. For students who may be a member of the racial majority and the religious minority and vice versa, their identity is divided. This multiplication and division makes the melting pot of the United States even more savory and complicated. Stewart and Lozano explain more succinctly:

> Experiences of marginalization may be multiplied (both identities are marginalized) or divided (one identity is marginalized and the other is not) depending on the particular ways in which individuals identify racially/ ethnically and religiously.... As such, religious identity may not be seen as a separate identity facet at all, but rather as one aspect of how they make meaning of their racial/ethnic identities.
>
> (Stewart & Lozano, 2009, p. 23)

Some religious minorities, based on their dress and physical appearance, have the opportunity to make choices about when, how, where, or whether to reveal their religious identity. Depending on their race and the decision to wear religious clothing, they might not be identified as a religious minority. Conversely, it may be assumed that a person is a religious minority because of their race. These are examples of how religious identity can be intertwined with racial identity. Race and traditional western clothing can be somewhat of a disguise for religious minority students, especially if there are no safe spaces on campus.

The concept of privilege was first discussed in relation to race by Peggy McIntosh in 1989. The difference between race and religion is that one generally does not choose their race, though individuals have chosen to "pass" from one race to another, while one is typically raised in a certain religious faith or decides to convert to a particular belief system. Bowman and Smedley (2013) make other distinctions between race and religion.

> While there are important parallels between religious and racial/ethnic minority status, these social categories are not perfectly analogous. First, race and ethnicity are often readily apparent in face-to-face interpersonal interactions, whereas this is often not the case for religious identification. Visible and invisible forms of minority status are associated with a different (although somewhat overlapping) set of interpersonal concerns and psychological stressors.
>
> (p. 748)

Moreover, racial categories may differ depending on the country or historical era. For example, slavery and Jim Crow in the United States enforced the one drop rule, meaning one drop of Negro or "Colored" blood meant a person was Black. Specifically, if a person had one Black great-grandparent, they were considered Black, Colored or Negro. In other countries, such as Brazil and South Africa, a person of mixed parentage is considered Brown (not Black) in Brazil or Colored in South Africa. Religious categories are consistent internationally – a Hindu in India is a Hindu in the United States. However, individuals can change their religious affiliation by converting to another religion or belief system. Also, it is unlikely that religious minorities face negative or positive stereotypes in regard to their academic ability as Asian, Hispanic, or Black students might. Christianity certainly has benefits for its adherents of color in the United States: "Membership in almost any Christian group eases the way for participation in a wide range of social and civic institutions, thus conferring privilege because of the similarities between Christian world views and civic calendars and social norms" (Fried, 2007).

Historically, the treatment of Jews walked a thin line between racial and religious discrimination. Though Jews are considered White, this ethnic group was discriminated against in the form of quotas for university admissions. Elite universities such as Harvard, Dartmouth, and Yale instituted quotas to limit the number of Jewish students enrolled (Buchsbaum, 1987). Anti-Jewish quotas peaked during the 1920s and 1930s. The practice of limiting the number of Jewish students declined after World War II and ceased during the 1950s (Lavender, 1977). The president of Dartmouth at the time, President

129

Hopkins, justified the Jewish quota by proclaiming Dartmouth a Christian college founded to Christianize students (Buschbaum, 1987, p. 82). The history of Jewish admissions quotas is just one example of the history and traditions student affairs practitioners should understand when approaching religious diversity. Institutions can't know where they're going if they don't know where they've been.

Researchers have linked ethnic identity to spirituality. According to Chae, Kelly, Brown, and Bolden (2004), ethnic identity is positively correlated with spiritual ends and means. The following definitions are appropriate to explain the aforementioned research results. Ethnic identity is defined as the designation by ethnic minority group members of their own distinct sub-culture from the dominant culture. Spiritual means emphasizing the process of developing harmony and connectedness with the sacred or divine, while spiritual ends refers to the goals one aspires to reach within an organization or faith in order to receive social status or material gain (Chae et al., 2004, pp. 17–18). Students with a strong ethnic identity may have different spiritual needs from those with a less distinct ethnic identity.

Additional research has explored White racial identity development and religious orientation. Sciarra and Gushue (2003) use Helms' (1995) six White racial identity ego statuses (contact, disintegration, reintegration, pseudo-independence, immersion/emersion, and autonomy) to demonstrate how White identity manifests in a religious context. The term status is used, instead of stage, because stage implies a place that one reaches one at a time in a certain order, whereas statuses are not mutually exclusive and can be attained in any order.

Contact status holders believe racism only occurs outside of his or her religious community and blindly accept religious teachings. Disintegration status holders are discontent with discrepancies between a religious tradition's hiring practices and its public statements. Reintegration status holders support a theology of suffering, believing happiness is supposed to come in the next life. Reintegration status holders also believe other religious traditions are flawed. Pseudo-independence status holders are dedicated to serving the less fortunate and oppose dogmatic expressions of faith. Immersion/emersion status holders are questioning their own beliefs and seeking a new community away from their own religious tradition. Autonomy status holders support inclusion within their religious community and are open to insights from other faiths. Also, they are aware of the strengths and weaknesses of their own religious tradition. Student affairs professionals' understanding of these statuses and their implications for religion can enhance interreligious and interracial interactions on campus.

As student affairs practitioners work to meet the needs of religious minorities, the religious minority experience may be more useful than knowledge of rituals attributed to a certain faith. Sciarra and Gushue (2003) explain: "Both racial identity theorists and psychologists of religion have concluded that mere factual knowledge regarding a client's race or religion is of limited heuristic value for the counseling process" (p. 480). Moreover, understanding students' racial perspectives can help college personnel understand their religious perspectives and viewpoints.

Using Fouad and Brown's (2000) definition of ethnic group, Schlosser (2003) argues that religion can also be considered an ethnic group. Fouad and Brown define ethnic group as a group of people who live or once lived in close proximity to one another and share ways of thinking, feeling, and behaving, learning from similar life circumstances shared over generations (p. 381). This definition certainly applies to religious groups. However, the argument that religion is an ethnic group overlooks the convert experience. Though persons in the same ethnic group often share the same faith, there are Black Jews and White Muslim converts in the United States. Convert is defined as someone who has converted to a religion or spiritual background different from their childhood. Just because tenets of a particular faith appeal to you does not mean you live, or once lived, in close proximity or share ways of thinking, feeling, and behaving from similar life circumstances. In fact, those of the same faith can have quite different generational life experiences. One example is Arab-American Muslims and Black/African-American Muslims. Though these groups share a faith, their experiences as ethnic groups are different. African-American Muslims are a sizeable Muslim convert demographic, comprising the majority of Muslims born in the United States (Pew Center, 2011).

SUGGESTIONS FOR RESEARCH

Future research should explore students' opinions about religious minority faculty. Watt (2007) argues that it is difficult for students to separate their learning experiences from their opinions of their professor. Specifically, research should explore the course evaluations of religious minority faculty. Instructors belonging to minority or disadvantaged groups receive lower course evaluations than their counterparts. Researchers should explore if this is true for religious minority college instructors.

Occurrences of religious conflict and religiously motivated hate crimes and aggressions should be researched. Specifically, the rates of these types of incidents should be recorded. Existing research demonstrates that racial incidents are underreported (Hurtado & Ruiz, 2012). Future research should explore if the same is true for religiously motivated incidents. According to Hurtado and Ruiz's (2012) research, a majority of students of color reported that racist verbal comments were the most prevalent form of discrimination they

131

experienced. Future research should explore if this is also true for religious minorities.

Future research should also explore Greek life for religious minorities. As discussed in Chapter 5, the legacy of Jewish fraternities and sororities and the recent organization of Muslim Greek organizations provide an opportunity for religious minorities to engage in campus life. Religious minority fraternities and sororities can assist student affairs practitioners in understanding historical perspectives of religious oppression. Considering the major role of athletics on college campus and the increasing popularity of evangelical Christian student athlete organizations (DeBerg, 2002), future research should explore the experiences of religious minority athletes and any proliferation of religious minority organizations for college athletes. According to Small and Bowman (2013), more research is needed on how religious minority students may experience religious transformation. Future research should explore religious diversity among student affairs professionals and how to recruit more religious minorities to the profession. This will help students interact with staff from the same religious backgrounds. Images and experiences are important. Students need to see practitioners that believe as they do. Future research needs to examine the religious perspectives of student affairs professionals. Are student affairs professionals as a demographic prone to being more secular, religious, or spiritual? Once researchers explore majority and minority religious groups the way race and gender are examined, society will enjoy a greater understanding of religious group differences (Schlosser, 2003). Though this text is aimed at student affairs practitioners, research is important because research is what will inform the practice.

COMPETENCIES FOR STUDENT AFFAIRS PROFESSIONALS

The National Association of Student Personnel Administrators' (NASPA) knowledge community on religion and spirituality in higher education and the American College Student Personnel Association's (ACPA) Commission for Spirituality, Faith, Religion, and Meaning (CSFRM) collaborated to develop competencies addressing spirituality, secularism, religious pluralism, and interfaith cooperation within student affairs. These are the proposed competencies for student affairs professionals.

Student affairs professionals:

Can demonstrate awareness and respect regarding the difference between spirituality, religiosity, and secularism, recognizing the distinctions as well as the integration of these concepts and how they impact the lives of individuals in society.

Are knowledgeable regarding world religions, humanistic worldviews, and diverse spiritual perspectives and, when lacking information, actively seek out resources and professionals with such expertise.

Are cognizant of how spirituality, religion, and secularism can shape identity development and meaning making, both individually and collectively.

Recognize the impact that religious privilege has on campus regarding issues such as the academic calendar, official campus holidays, programming, and religious/spiritual visibility and strive to challenge the pervasive reach of dominant spiritual, religious, or secular traditions.

Are aware of how their own worldview, values, biases, and perceptions about religious, spiritual, or secular traditions may impact the helping relationship and seek supervision and consultation when faced with hindrances to effective practice.

Recognize their own limitations and lack of knowledge regarding spiritual, religious, or secular traditions and collaborate with campus chaplains/ministers, community leaders/elders, healers, teachers, and other resources in providing information that supports the needs of students, faculty, and staff.

Seek to ensure that students, faculty, staff and guests have a respectful and appropriate space on campus devoted to meditation, prayer, solace, and quiet reflection.

Actively seek ways to foster constructive, meaningful, and pluralistic dialogues on campus concerning pathways to understanding purpose and meaning making, including religious, spiritual, and secular perspectives, especially traditions, world philosophies, or beliefs that are underrepresented or marginalized.

Are prepared to assist students, faculty, and staff during spiritual or existential crises and spiritual identity development milestones by providing appropriate support, resources, and referrals that meet the spiritual, secular, or religious needs of the campus.

Recognize the intersection of spiritual, secular, and religious identity with other aspects of students' cultural identities, such as race, ethnicity, and gender, sexual/gender identity, socioeconomic status, (dis)ability, and other underrepresented cultural markers.

133

Demonstrate the skills necessary to effectively assess the needs of students, faculty, staff, and campus constituents as they develop purpose and meaning in their lives, regardless of the religious, spiritual, or secular approach they embrace.

Continually seek to enhance their own development regarding spirituality, secularism, religion, and meaning making; clarify their beliefs and values; and gain increasingly complex and nuanced understanding of their own chosen pathway to meaning and purpose and its application to their personal and vocational lives.

(Kocet & Stewart, 2011)

These competencies encourage the professional, as well as personal, growth required for student affairs professionals to meet the needs of all students, regardless of their religious background.

The future for interfaith work and religious minorities on college campuses is promising. Elizabethtown College in Pennsylvania is the first institution to offer a major in interfaith studies (Elizabethtown College, 2015). The program aspires to prepare skilled professionals for a world of diverse perspectives and beliefs. Programs such as this can prepare prospective student affairs practitioners to implement interfaith programming and religious pluralism awareness. The first accredited Islamic-affiliated college in the United States is Zaytuna College, founded in 1996. Offering a Bachelor's degree in Islamic Law and Theology, Zaytuna conferred its first degrees in 2014 (Zaytuna College, 2015). Located in Berkeley, California, Zaytuna adds to the diversity of religiously affiliated colleges in the United States. The future landscape for religious minorities in higher education is changing positively.

Students must be prepared to thrive in environments with people of diverse religious backgrounds. Being exposed to diversity doesn't mean that students have explored their identity within that diversity or what it means to be engaged in a diverse community. In other words, being exposed to non-Christians doesn't mean that Christians understand what it means to truly be engaged with others who are not Christian. College campuses are, arguably, microcosms of the world. Ideally, the wealthy, the disadvantaged, all races, religions would be represented on college campuses. Our future great minds are in college somewhere today. The nature of the institutional climate, opportunities for learning about other religions, and interfaith practices among faculty and staff are key features of a religiously inclusive learning environment that result in developing informed and engaged citizens. Let the progress brought by interfaith cooperation spread beyond college campuses, beyond the ivory tower, into every level and space of society. College students are our future leaders. Religious freedom is the impetus for the founding of this country. Religious freedom can also be an impetus for increased student engagement and satisfaction on college campuses across the United States.

REFERENCES

Allen, K.E., & Kellom, G.E. (2001). The role of spirituality in student affairs and staff development. *New Directions for Student Services, 95,* 47–55.

Baltazar, T., & Coffen, R. (2011). The role of doubt in religious identity development and psychological maturity. *Journal of Research on Christian Education, 20,* 182–194.

Bowman, N.A., & Smedley, C.T. (2013). The forgotten minority: Examining religious affiliation and university satisfaction. *Higher Education, 65,* 745–760.

Bryant, A.N., & Astin, H.S. (2008). The correlates of spiritual struggle during the college years. *Journal Of Higher Education, 79*(1), 1–27.

Buchsbaum, T. (1987). A note on antisemitism in admissions at Dartmouth. *Jewish Social Studies, 49*(1), 79–84.

Chae, M.H., Kelly, D.B., Brown, C.F., & Bolden, M.A. (2004). Relationship of ethnic identity and spiritual development: An exploratory study. *Counseling and Values, 49,* 15–26.

DeBerg, B.A. (2002). Athletes and religion on campus. *Peer Review, 4*(4), 10.

Elizabethtown College. (2015). *Interfaith Leadership Studies.* Retrieved from www.etown.edu/depts/religious-studies/ILShome.aspx.

Fisherman, S. (2002). Spiritual identity in Israeli religious male adolescents: Observations and educational implications. *Religious Education, 97*(1), 61–79.

Fouad, N.A., & Brown, M. (2000). Race, ethnicity, culture, class and human development. In S.D. Brown & R.W. Lent (eds) *Handbook of Counseling Psychology* (3rd edn). New York: Wiley.

Fried, J. (2007, Summer). Religious privilege: Dialogue or domination? *Developments, 5*(2). Retrieved from www.myacpa.org/publications/developments/volume-5-issue-2.

Goodman, K.M., & Mueller, J.A. (2009). Invisible, marginalized, and stigmatized: Understanding the needs of Atheist students. *New Directions for Student Services, 125,* 55–63.

Helms, J.E. (1995) An update of Helm's White and people of color racial identity models. In J.G. Ponterotto, J.M. Casas, & C.M. Alexander (eds) *Handbook of Multicultural Counseling.* Thousand Oaks, CA: Sage.

Hollinger, D.A. (2002). Enough already: Universities do not need more Christianity. In A. Sterk (ed.) *Religion, Scholarship, & Higher Education: Perspectives, Models, and Future Prospects.* Notre Dame, IN: Notre Dame Press.

Hurtado, S., & Ruiz, A. (2012). *The Climate for Underrepresented Groups and Diversity on Campus*. Los Angeles, CA: Higher Education Research Institute.

Kazanjian, V., Keen, J., & Laurence, P. (2010). Building a new global commons: Religious diversity and the challenge for higher education. *Journal of Interreligious Dialogue, 4*, 29–37.

Kocet, M.M., & Stewart, D.L. (2011). The role of student affairs in promoting religious and secular pluralism and interfaith cooperation. *Journal of College and Character, 12*(1) (Online). doi: 10.22202/1940–1639.1762.

Lavender, A.D. (1977). Studies of Jewish college students: A review and a replication. *Jewish Social Studies, 39*(1/2), 37–52.

McIntosh, P. (1989, July/August). White privilege: Unpacking the invisible knapsack. *Peace and Freedom*. Retrieved from www.areteadventures.com/articles/white_privilege_unpacking_the_invisible_napsack.pdf.

Ortiz, A.M., & Rhoads, R.A. (2000). Deconstructing Whiteness as part of a multicultural education framework: From theory to practice. *Journal of College Student Development, 41*(1), 81–93.

Pew Center for the People and the Press. (2011). *Section 1: A Demographic Portrait of Muslim Americans*. Retrieved from www.people-press.org/2011/08/30/section-1-a-demographic-portrait-of-muslim-americans/.

Schlosser, L.Z. (2003). Christian privilege: Breaking a sacred taboo. *Journal of Multicultural Counseling and Development, 31*, 44–51.

Sciarra, D.T., & Gushue, G.V. (2003). White racial identity development and religious orientation. *Journal of Counseling and Development, 81*, 473–482.

Small, J.L. (2009). Faith dialogues foster identity development. *About Campus, 13*(6), 12–18.

Small, J.L., & Bowman, N.A. (2013). Religious commitment, skepticism, and struggle among U.S. college students: The impact of majority/minority religious affiliation and institutional type. *Journal for the Scientific Study of Religion, 50*(1), 154–174.

Sorrentino, P.V. (2010). What do college students want? A student centered approach to multifaith involvement. *Journal of Ecumenical Studies, 45*(1): 79–96.

Stewart, D.L., & Lozano, A. (2009). Difficult dialogues at the intersections of race, culture, and religion. *New Directions for Student Services, 125*, 23–31.

Sue, D.W., Bernier, J.E., Duran, A., Feinberg, L., Pederson, P., Smith, E.J., & Vasquez-Nuttal, E. (1982). Position paper: Cross-cultural counseling competencies. *The Counseling Psychologist, 10*(2), 45–52.

Tatum, B.D. (2000). The ABC approach to creating climates of engagement on diverse campuses. *Liberal Education, 86*(4), 22–29.

Watt, S.K. (2007). Difficult dialogues, privilege and social justice: Uses of the privileged identity exploration (PIE) model in student affairs practice. *College Student Affairs Journal, 26*(2), 114–126.

Woodrow, J. (2004). Institutional image: secular and marketing influences on Christian higher education. *Christian Higher Education, 3*(2), 115–125.

Young, G., & Davis-Russell, E. (2003). Dealing with difficult classroom dialogue. In P. Bronstein & K. Quina (eds) *Teaching Gender and Multicultural Awareness: Resources for the Psychology Classroom.* Washington, DC: American Psychological Association.

Zaytuna College. (2015). *A Brief History.* Retrieved from www.zaytuna.edu/about/.

Appendix A

U.S. Religious Knowledge Quiz

Angelo Pereira

The U.S. religious knowledge quiz (available online at http://www.pewforum.
org/quiz/u-s-religious-knowledge/) is a simple way to test the basic knowledge
of world religions. I liken it to knowing the basics of, say, Spanish or French.
As long as you paid some attention in class, or had a friend who spoke these
languages, you know the surface information of a more complex entity. Religions are so much deeper than the exterior face given to them by these questions. Yes, it is a good barometer to measure how much we pay attention to
other religions outside of our own, but it doesn't reflect knowledge or understanding of the subject matter. Everybody knows who Mother Teresa was, or
who Moses was, but how many people can say that they know all of the
fundamental teachings of a particular religion? These questions were common
knowledge questions. Yet, the majority of Americans who took this quiz only
answered one-third to two-thirds of them correctly. This was not surprising
to me, but it simply demonstrates the lack of knowledge of world religions in
a country dominated by Christianity.

I received a score of 15 out of 15, but that only comes from my elevated
interests in world cultures and history. Many of these questions were taught
or at least mentioned at some point in my life, but only those with a pure
interest retain and explore more into these facts. It would be interesting to
see how people of other countries score compared to us, as we are most often
seen as the more ignorant people of the world. What I found to be intriguing
is that atheists, or those who don't follow a particular religion, actually
scored higher than the average of quiz takers on 14 of the 15 religious questions. I wonder if this is because they have a broader horizon when it comes
to ideologies and beliefs. Typically, people of a given faith will not explore
others' faiths because they remain in the realm of their own beliefs, of course
believing them to be the only truths. The fact that atheists also answered
questions about Catholicism, Protestantism, and other religions better than
those who identify with those religions begs the question, how much do we
really know our own religions, let alone others?

138

Appendix B
Information Sheet Template

Study Title:
PI:
Date:

You are invited to participate in a research study conducted by Dr. _____________ from X University.

We are asking you to take part in this study because we wish to learn more about the experiences of American Animist, Buddhist, Hindu, Jewish or Muslim (select one) college students.

Your participation is voluntary and would consist of participating in an audio-recorded interview lasting approximately 45 minutes.

There are no anticipated risks to your participation and there are no direct benefits to you for taking part in this study. Thank you for your participation. You will be given a copy of this form.

If you have any further questions about this research study, please contact: Dr. _____________, University email address, Phone number

Appendix C
Interview Protocol

Interview caveat: Thank you for agreeing to participate in the current research study involving attitudes of students about being a religious minority on campus. I will proceed to ask you a series of questions regarding your experiences here at X University. Your feedback is important to us. Please note that all of your answers will be kept confidential and will remain anonymous. This means that there will be no way to link your name with your responses, which is one of the reasons your name is not requested. If at any time you are unclear about the particular question I am asking, please let me know so that I can clarify. I also wanted to let you know that there are no "right" or "wrong" answers. I am interested in your experience as a religious minority student on campus and I realize that this experience may be fundamentally different or perhaps similar to other students on campus. With that being said, let us begin.

1. What is your religious affiliation?
2. Please tell me your age, academic major, and grade point average?
3. Where are you originally from?
4. How would you rate your overall health? (Excellent, Very Good, Good, Fair, or Poor)
5. Are you a first generation college student?
6. Are you a transfer student? If so, when did you transfer to X University?
7. Do you live on or off campus?
8. Do you attend any on-campus or off-campus events? If yes, can you give me an example of the types of events/activities you like to participate in?
9. What are your reasons for attending X University?
10. Are you satisfied with your educational experience thus far?

11. What has been the most satisfying feature of your educational experience?

12. What has been the most unsatisfying feature of your educational experience?

13. How long have you been a Animist/Buddhist/Hindu/Jew/Muslim (select one)?

14. How has being a member of a religious minority affected your college experience?

15. Do you think the university does a good job catering to its Animist/Buddhist/Hindu/Jewish/Muslim (select one) students? Please elaborate and give specific examples.

16. What changes, if any, would you like to see on campus in order to accommodate Animist/Buddhist/Hindu/Jewish/Muslim (select one) students?

17. How important is it for you to maintain your Animist/Buddhist/Hindu/Jewish/Muslim (select one) identity on campus?

18. Are your friends primarily Animist/Buddhist/Hindu/Jewish/Muslim (select one) or a combination of different religious faiths?

19. For those persons on campus who happen to know you are Animist/Buddhist/Hindu/Jewish/Muslim (select one), how respectful would you say they are? (Very, Somewhat, or Not at All)

	Very Respectful	Somewhat Respectful	Not at All Respectful
X University administration			
Faculty			
Staff			
X University students			
Friends			
Roommate(s)			
Family members			
Local residents			

20. On average, how knowledgeable would you say the following individuals are about your religion? (Very, Somewhat, Not at All)

	Very Knowledgeable	Somewhat Knowledgeable	Not at All Knowledgeable
X University administration			
Faculty			
Staff			
X University students			
Friends			
Roommate(s)			
Family members			
Local residents			

21. In the future, would you send your children to X University? Why or why not?

Ending caveat: We have reached the conclusion of our interview. Is there anything that you would like to add to anything that has already been said? Is there anyone else that you think would be interested in participating in the current study? If yes, please provide contact information so that they can be reached.

I wish you the best during the remainder of your matriculation at X University. Thank you for participating once again.

Appendix D
Actual Student Interview Transcript

All names in the following transcript are pseudonyms.

Interviewee "A": Muslim male college student who attends an HBCU in the United States.

Okay, what is your major. Well, you told me your major is math so what is your classification?
Senior.
And how old are you?
21
Okay, great!
I turn 22 April 20th.
And you graduate in May? Wonderful. And what is your GPA?
3.52 currently, overall.
Where were you born?
Indianapolis, IN.
Is that where you're from?
I was born in Indianapolis, IN and raised in Atlanta.
Okay.
There are nine of us and I'm number four.
So there are nine of you and you're number four?
That's right.
Wow. You were born in Indianapolis, raised in Atlanta. So when did you come to Houston?
I came to Houston in 2009. I got married and came to Houston.
And did you transfer here or did you start school somewhere else?
I started school here.
And where were your parents born?

Mom was born in New York and my dad was born ... I'm not sure where my dad was born.

But he was born in the U.S.?

Yes, he was born in the U.S., I think he was born in Georgia or Florida.

How do you identify yourself racially or ethnically?

African-American.

How would you describe your overall health?

Good.

Did your parents go to college? Are they college graduates?

Yes.

Where did they graduate from?

My mom graduated from Emory. Well, I think she graduated IUPUI first and got her master's in math from Emory. And my dad got his master's in math from IUPUI. Or maybe it's the other way around. I think my mom got her master's from Emory. Both of my parents have master's degrees in math.

And you did not transfer here?

Correct.

I'm assuming you live off campus?

Yes.

Just you and your wife?

And we just had a baby.

So you have one or two?

We just have one.

A little girl?

Yes, one year old.

So you live in an apartment?

Yes.

Is that how you lived since you came here and got married?

Right, we've always had an apartment. I did stay on campus the summer when I came for the math program, the scholarship program I'm in. So that was like the only time that summer I stayed with incoming freshmen in that program. Then, after that I stayed off campus.

How far do you live from campus?

About 5–10 minutes.

So you've been married your whole time as a student?

Yes.

What extracurricular activities do you participate in?

On campus?

Yes.

None.

Why, or is there a reason why?

Yes, there is a reason. There is no male soccer team. But if they did I would have been playing.

Did you look for a school with a soccer team?

It wasn't a major thing. I knew I was coming to TSU. I knew U of H had a soccer team when I was in Atlanta so I was applying to that, but the deciding factor was the scholarship program.

In math.

I got a scholarship to come to TSU in math.

Without the scholarship would you have wanted to come here?

Without the scholarship, I would have come to Houston still, because I was getting married, but I probably would have gone to U of H because they had a soccer team and a good math program.

Is Rasheeda [his wife] a student here?

She is a student here so I probably would have still come.

So I can interview her?

She already graduated.

Okay.

So she is a year ahead of me so she would have had to come to Atlanta.

Right, she was in school still.

So I probably would have come to TSU anyway.

So there was a period when you two were in school together.

Yes.

What community activities off campus, unrelated to campus, do you participate in?

I do the math and chess club and the masjid I attend, Warithdeen Muhammed.

What are your hobbies other than soccer and chess? Or would you consider those your hobbies?

Yes, soccer, chess, math, all sports really, tennis and just working with the youth in the community.

How satisfied are you with your college experience?

Highly satisfied, very satisfied.

What makes it highly satisfying?

The mathematics department at TSU.

What is it about the mathematics department that makes it satisfying?

One, the success that they have achieved as far as African-Americans in mathematics. Two males in our department both graduated from U of H's Ph.D. in mathematics program. And I think there are only a total of three or four (African-Americans) in the whole history [of U of H]. Two, the way they are able to relay information and they accept students as far as they invest in students a lot. The opportunities that my wife and I have now to further our education is based on what the math department has done. And the scholarship program which is tied in with the math department, so those two (math department and scholarship program) made my experience here just amazing.

Any dissatisfying things in your experience here?

No, nothing major, just dealing with professors that you may not like but nothing major.

So you were raised Muslim?

Yes, third generation.

How do you think being Muslim has impacted your college experience?

I think it has allowed me to stay focused and come to school with an understanding of purpose for why I'm here to get in and not get distracted. And I think my professors noticed that which was amazing because we have a lot of African-American females come here but I was like one out of [many other students] and I received the award for outstanding mathematician in the department. So when I leave they are kinda sad because we really don't have many more males coming in. But I attribute [my performance] to the way I was raised as far as being Muslim and staying focused on what you're here for.

What did Rasheeda study?

Mathematics. She started out in chemistry, then switched to mathematics. So we both actually, we've applied and been accepted to the Ph.D. program at the University of Iowa and that was done from the networking of professors on our behalf here.

Wonderful.

At a big university, you know, you don't actually get the personal attention of professors. So that's why my brother, he went to Howard, and when I was asking him should I go to the Mathews University [local PWI] and he was telling me at an HBCU you'll get the personal attention and you will have quality professors. It's been a blessing that our math department is top quality and they were able to make connections as far as making things happen for us.

So you are going to start in the fall?

Right.

So how good of a job do you think Texas Southern does in meeting the needs of its Muslim students?

I would say not good but my opinion is probably biased because I'm not always on campus. For a period, I and my wife and her sister and another brother we established a Muslim organization for students on campus. It was here for about two years. That was the period when we were all here [enrolled]. When my wife and her sister graduated and the other brother transferred, it was only me. We were trying to establish different things on campus. The main thing we wanted to get was a prayer room. I know we were all busy but I would say before that I would say that was the only thing we weren't able to get established.

So what were the roadblocks or why weren't you able to get a prayer room?

I will say it was our lack of knowledge of how to get a prayer room. That's first. So, it's not all on TSU. We tried, I know we spoke with our advisor.

Who is your advisor?

Dr. Nasif, she was the advisor. We were trying to get a room in the rec center but we were told it had to be more of a silent room, not just for Muslims, it had to be so anyone could use it. There was a lot about getting it done that we didn't know at first. That's one thing that would be for future generations I think it would be good for them to have somewhere they can go and make prayer.

So would you say it was more you just kinda went up against that and dropped it? You weren't told no.

We weren't told no.

I know where I got my doctorate, we had a prayer room but it was advertised as a meditation room but we were the only ones who used it. And there was no furniture … I think it was bigger than this, a little bigger than this [motions around the diameter of the room], you know, a small room so that's basically it and this was a public university and Texas Southern is public.

So any changes you would like to see would be a prayer room. Any other changes?

That is the only one I can think of.

So what would you say it is like and I know you've only gone to school here but what would you say it's like being a Muslim student at an HBCU?

I think you really have to be grounded in Islam, your foundation as far as … [voice trails off].

No judgment.

At every school you have distractions. For me it was a blessing that I stayed off campus and I did a lot of things in the science building. Just in general you have a lot of different … I can't think of a word for it … mentalities, I guess I can say, openness of different students and their way of dressing. I know that's a big one but it's funny because throughout my experience I really haven't had that many encounters with a lot of different [people].

Because you live off campus?

Right.

When I went to take my graduation pictures, right when they snapped the pictures there was a fight, and they go to U of M, you know Lisa and Akbar Musa.

I don't know many people, I just moved here, I've been to the masjid a few times but I don't really know anybody.

Oh, okay, well they were there and there was a fight and they were like "seriously" and I was like that is the first fight I've seen.

They were fighting?

Yeah, it was someone else fighting.

Inside?

Well it was right outside where we were taking pictures but it was ironic because I've never seen a fight here but U of M comes and it's like "wow" so they have the wrong impression.

How integrated would you say Muslim students are into campus life?

I would say not very integrated.

How important is it for you to maintain your Muslim identity on campus?

You said how important?

Yes.

I think it's very important.

Are your friends here primarily Muslim or a combination of both Muslim and Christian?

A combination of both but primarily I guess Christian.

How do you think your experience would be different if you attended another university?

Under the same circumstances, I think it would be about the same or I don't think it would be much better. I primarily stick to the math department. I rarely ventured out. That's why I say not that integrated because I did the whole math club but as far as the TSU spring break goes I attended and got some food but I didn't really, you know, participate and volunteer too much.

How would you describe relationships and interactions between Muslim students and non-Muslim faculty, staff, and administrators?

From my experience, everything has been okay. There are different things that happen over the years like you have a lot of jokes come out. Or some statements but faculty is good but some students they say things that are annoying but in conversation with each other and you may happen to be around but rarely have I seen that from faculty.

What kinds of things have you heard students say?

I'm trying to think of the most recent. Oh, the most recent was I don't think directed toward anything that's happened in the U.S. but they were more so just talking up Christianity and talking down Islam I guess you could say to another Christian. So one Christian was saying you have Buddhism, you have Islam and the other person was just talking about Christianity.

So they were just more promoting Christianity, it wasn't like they said anything offensive.

Well, in the conversation I guess some things were offensive. Well, I guess I shouldn't say offensive but not derogatory. Yes, not derogatory.

How would you describe your level of religious practice?

You said how would I describe the level?

Yes, your level.

I think it's okay. I think it could be better but I think I would say it's good.

How knowledgeable would you say faculty and staff and other students are about Islam?

Not knowledgeable.

Would you send your child to Texas Southern?

I would but a lot of professors are leaving but if she was going through the same scenario [as I] then yes because one professor was really my mentor and he's staying so I've been telling him I've got my daughter but that was a joke because they're [the professors] are old. So he was moving on so I was joking with him but it depends on how the scenario goes. But without the math department, I probably wouldn't.

How tolerant and inclusive do you think the campus environment is toward Muslim students?

I think they are tolerant. I think it's tolerant.

Would you say its inclusive?

In the fact of us being here, I guess you could say its inclusive.

Well, you can tolerate something you don't really like. But I don't want to answer for you.

I mean when you say inclusive, I'm thinking in my head as far as inclusive is there halal food, then that would be no.

So maybe tolerant but not inclusive?

Right.

How would you say being a student at Texas Southern has impacted your religious practice and faith?

That's a good one, can you repeat that?

How would you say being a student at Texas Southern has impacted your religious practice and faith?

I would think that its impact would depend upon the person to person as far as I see the different things you encounter I see as a challenge but you make the challenge to better you as a person. So I haven't really seen it stand on the same foundation we stand on as Muslims but whatever you're dealing with it just makes you a better person.

I wanna talk a little bit about when you and Rasheeda were both in school married, so one of the reasons we ask if you're married or engaged is because we know how important marriage is to Muslims and being on campus in a college environment – what was that like for the two of you being married? Can you talk a little bit about that?

A lot of people – that usually was one thing that got a lot of people's attention. They were always wondering why or what was the reason or something like that but as far as us that in itself on top of the math department helped us to stay focused even more. You can have school but you still need to have a social life. It was much easier for us to socialize in groups with friends knowing that we're married.

Friends that were Texas Southern students?

Yes, that were Texas Southern students. So a lot of time when sisters come across and engage me in conversation they'll find out I was married and they'll be like "oh" so whatever their intent was...

Oh, you mean other women?

Right, in our college department.

To give you the story, I was in the lab one time and it was like during the summer and basically they didn't know I was married at that particular time because we'd just got married or I think we were getting married ... basically she had just come in [the lab], she [his wife] was already in the program and she was at the computer and they saw me talking past them to her and they were like "you know her" and I was like yeah that's my wife and then they were like "okay" so a lot of them were shocked.

So if you had a child that didn't want to study math, you wouldn't send her here.

Right.

What kind of school would you like to send her to?

I would like us to have a Muslim university. But it doesn't have to be. But it would be nice for one I would like to be a part of it as far as the level of education you get but also the level of things you can do toward religious focus and not deal with all of that. That would be nice. An American Muslim university, so not going overseas or anything like that. It doesn't only have to be Muslims. I guess I would say a university that is more inclusive of Muslims.

Give me some concrete examples ... prayer room, you mentioned halal food. What are some other things you would like to see? If your daughter was going to college ... other than academic programs?

A university that had faculty, not faculty, administrators that were Muslim, we could actually have a president or a highest level provost or things like that where you have people kind of like the U.S. government has like a director of international affairs or interfaith affairs and interfaith dialogue as far as actually having that. And a presence from each and every community. Administrators who are Muslim, not just faculty. More interfaith dialogue. That would be nice.

There are some schools that have that [interfaith dialogue].

I didn't do much research.

Well, maybe not here in Houston, I'm just saying in general, not saying you should have gone there.

Right, I understand. I think the major thing is if the Muslims don't have a presence then as a parent ... I know my sisters [are in school] in Atlanta, and they stay at home because the campus is not conducive for their betterment. If I was on campus I would have been challenged a lot more as far as many different challenges, people bothering you, coming at you, [dis]respecting you because I know my wife she did a year here without me so was on campus so she could probably answer a lot more questions than I can.

Is she from here?

Yes, she's from Houston. I don't know if she could do the interview, I could let her know. She asked.

No, it has to be a current student.

Yeah, but some of the stories she had was just her roommate bringing in people, which is bothersome.

Do you know any Muslims who are not African-American who are on campus?

Yes, I know a couple. Some I know from being in classes, but I don't talk to them like that. Actually one good one I know, he's from Eritrea. His parents are from Eritrea, I think he was born here. His name is Usman and he was in our association and he came with me to the summer program that summer. The scholarship program was very respectful and they actually grouped me with another Muslim student. I think something happened and he didn't come back this semester. I think it was funding but I think he'll be back next semester. But he was born here and he could tell you a lot because he's not married and he lived on campus and I've seen the transition from being with over the summer into things he was getting into.

Schools are supposed to meet the needs of all students if they're on campus. In one of my classes we talked about why there is no graduate or family housing here and there are students that could take advantage of that.

I know one problem he had was that they were trying to make him room with a person who was not heterosexual. So he was trying to get out of that. He was upset. So different things like that ... When you step outside of the math program we were in, which he had to do, you run into a lot more problems.

So you feel like the math department sort of gave you a bubble?

Yes.

Would you and Rasheeda have wanted to live on campus if there was family housing available?

Probably not. One, because it would have cost a lot more to live on campus. And deal with whatever the draw is on campus that it would probably not be worth it.

Anything else?

I really enjoyed my experience at Texas Southern. and I really love TSU. And my brother was telling me that you have people that go to HBCUs that have really good experiences and you have people that don't. So it really just depends on what you get when you get there and what you're going for. The fact that we were going for math and the math department is just extraordinary was a blessing.

Index

Page numbers in *italics* denote tables, those in **bold** denote figures.